"Isaiah Hankel has written an absurdly motiva[...] so motivational, I was constantly tempted to p[...] start getting things done using Hankel's strateg[...] able in the best possible way. But I always came back for more of Isaiah Hankel's wisdom—and the wisdom he distills from Einstein, Ben Franklin and even *The Shawshank Redemption*."

AJ Jacobs, Author of Four *New York Times* Bestselling Books;
Editor at Large, *Esquire Magazine*

"*Black Hole Focus* is a wake up call for anyone who feels stuck, distracted, or lost in their own life. Isaiah lays out very actionable steps for taking control of your future and setting yourself up for certain victory. This book will show you how to think like an entrepreneur and develop the mindset necessary for achieving your biggest dreams."

Lewis Howes, Former Professional Football Player and
Host of The School of Greatness

"Be careful if you read this book. Through interesting stories, compelling case studies and his own inspiring journey, Hankel demolishes your excuses and lays out a plan to identify and fulfill your life's purpose."

Clay Herbert, Founder of Crowdfunding Hacks and Spindows;
The Mastermind Behind Over 35 Successful Kickstarters

"*Black Hole Focus* is your road map to transformation in ways most have never even dared to dream. If you want to go from merely living a life to becoming the hero in your own adventure, start here. Hankel's words jump off the page, swat you on the backside, pierce your heart, and take you on a ride into a magical journey of your own design! Brilliant in its brunt, dazzling in its denouement, triumphant in its precision, this is one of the most important books you will ever read. Prepare to be transformed!"

Dr Gina Loudon, Fox News Contributor and Syndicated Host of
SmartLife; Author of *What Women REALLY Want*

"As a memory champion, I realize just how important it is to harness your mental energy and focus it in a way that helps you to achieve your goals. I'm very impressed with Black Hole Focus and strongly believe that it can help you learn to harness your mental energy and focus it like a laser in order to achieve incredible success in business and personal endeavors."

Chester Santos, US Memory Champion;
"The International Man of Memory"

"In fighting and in life, focus is what separates winners from losers. Focus is what helped me win the UFC TUF Championship. Any successful mixed martial artist will tell you that seeing yourself as a champion is the first step to becoming a champion. You have to start with a vision. You have to start at the end. That's why I love this book, because it tells you to start at the end and work backwards. *Black Hole Focus* is an amazing read because it helps people create a vision for their lives and then it shows them how to achieve their vision. The book makes you see yourself at the top of the podium and then it gives you a detailed training plan to help you get there. If you want to be a champion, buy this book. *Black Hole Focus* will show you how to win."

Michael "Maverick" Chiesa, Mixed Martial Artist and UFC TUF Champion

"Isaiah demonstrates a powerful lesson, that we are all masters of our own destiny. His book provides practical and, more importantly, actionable advice on how to reach our most important goals while consistently achieving lifelong career and personal satisfaction. Early career scientists would especially benefit from its stepwise, methodical approach to fearless self-examination and keen demonstration of an intensely focused purpose. The chapters on storytelling strike at the heart of the of the dilemma most scientists and professionals have, that they are impostors in their own field and are undeserving of happiness and accolades. As Isaiah explains, this couldn't be further from the truth once you recognize the lessons to be learned from past incidents and begin to tell a new story of perseverance and accomplishment."

James Gould, PhD, Director of Harvard Medical School Office for Postdoctoral Fellows

"A brilliantly written step-by-step process to help you learn what you really want in life and exactly how to get it. Read this book if you want to get focused, find your purpose and change your life."

Jacqueline Biggs, Author of the International Bestseller *Marketing to Win*

"*Black Hole Focus* is exceptionally well written and the examples found throughout the book are terrific in showing the reader how to quickly implement each concept. Isaiah shares very engaging personal stories, striking the right balance in showing his humanity without coming being overly instructive."

Matthew Kissner, Wiley Board of Directors; CEO of The Kissner Group

"Stuck! That was the word echoing in my head. I was trapped in a difficult career decision and unable to focus on what I really wanted. That's when *Black Hole Focus* sucked me in. I seriously couldn't put it down. I remember sitting up late one night flipping through chapter after chapter and then writing out a 10-page list of my biggest dreams and "daily actions." I was more inspired than I've ever been. But that wasn't the best part. The best part was that this book gave me an action plan for achieving my goals. It showed me how to find my purpose and then it showed me how to fulfill it. *Black Hole Focus* has been a game-changer for me."

Sabine Bois, Former CEO of SAW Instruments; CFO of Occlutech Holding AG

"*Black Hole Focus* is incredibly powerful. Isaiah magically combines personal stories, case studies, and scientific data to create an compelling and life-changing book. Isaiah is so open and so vulnerable that you can't help but feel a sense of security, trust, and inspiration all at once as you read. I've never read a book that so clearly defined how to make a lasting change in your life. This book will knock you right out of your chair—you'll be sucked into a new way of thinking and a new way of living. *Black Hole Focus* is intellectual, entertaining, and personal. It's the kind of book that you wait your whole life to read."

Melis Zararsız, Managing Editor of Beyazperde.com

"If you've been searching for the key that unlocks the real secret to a fulfilling and successful life, then you've picked up the right book at the right time. I have been involved in personal development for over 20 years, dedicated to changing lives and helping people achieve greatness. Throughout this time I have been able to study people up close. One thing that stands out is that all successful people possess a powerful purpose. Each of us has greatness just waiting to be recognized and tapped into. In *Black Hole Focus*, Isaiah provides you with the step-by-step process to unlocking your greatness.

"Isaiah sets out in simple steps what needs to be done. He walks his talk. He lives his purpose and lives a life most people would envy. He proves that anyone, from anywhere, can be truly successful no matter what their past or where they began.

"He gives you the tools to experience life to its fullest by discovering your true potential, uncovering your passion and igniting the desire to make a difference to the world. As you read this book, take note of Isaiah's advice, trust the process and immediately follow his directions at the end of each chapter. Then be ready for the miraculous transformation that happens in your life.

"If you are serious about living life to it's fullest, the book you are holding can take you there. Begin your journey now and reap the rewards it has to offer. This is a start of a new beginning."

Joh Graney, Managing Director of Joh Graney Leadership Systems and Author of *Painting the Dream*

"*Black Hole Focus* reveals a concrete methodology for creating a powerful purpose through structured and comprehensive steps, wittily described in short and clear paragraphs, and sensibly illustrated with personal examples and case studies from several successful people. This book is a required reading for anyone committed to achieving greatness in life."

Elison Matioli, PhD, Research Scientist at Massachusetts Institute of Technology

"Isaiah Hankel is a powerhouse of ideas and ambitions. *Black Hole Focus* is an intense self-analysis without concern for collateral damage."

Adam Treister, Founder of Tree Star Inc. and Creator of FlowJo

"*Black Hole Focus* cuts to the chase while delivering huge value. Nailing your passion is not a nice to have, it's a must have and Isaiah helps you find and leverage it."

Craig Morantz, Co-Founder, President and COO Shifthub; Investor and Marketing Advisor at CrowdCare Corporation

Black Hole Focus

How Intelligent People Can Create a Powerful Purpose for Their Lives

Isaiah Hankel, PhD

CAPSTONE
A Wiley Brand

This edition first pu
© 2014 Isaiah Han
Registered office

John Wiley and So... The Atrium, Sou... ... Chichester, ...st Sussex, PO19 8SQ, United ...

For details of our g...obal editorial offices, for ... ...ormation about how to apply ...for permission to reuse the ...opyright material in this ...ok please see our website at www.wiley.com.

The right of the author to be identified as the author of this work has been asserted in accordance with the Copyright, Designs and Patents Act 1988.

All rights reserved. No part of this publication may be reproduced, stored in a retrieval system, or transmitted, in any form or by any means, electronic, mechanical, photocopying, recording or otherwise, except as permitted by the UK Copyright, Designs and Patents Act 1988, without the prior permission of the publisher.

Wiley publishes in a variety of print and electronic formats and by print-on-demand. Some material included with standard print versions of this book may not be included in e-books or in print-on-demand. If this book refers to media such as a CD or DVD that is not included in the version you purchased, you may download this material at http://booksupport.wiley.com. For more information about Wiley products, visit www.wiley.com.

Designations used by companies to distinguish their products are often claimed as trademarks. All brand names and product names used in this book and on its cover are trade names, service marks, trademarks or registered trademarks of their respective owners. The publisher and the book are not associated with any product or vendor mentioned in this book. None of the companies referenced within the book have endorsed the book.

Limit of Liability/Disclaimer of Warranty: While the publisher and author have used their best efforts in preparing this book, they make no representations or warranties with the respect to the accuracy or completeness of the contents of this book and specifically disclaim any implied warranties of merchantability or fitness for a particular purpose. It is sold on the understanding that the publisher is not engaged in rendering professional services and neither the publisher nor the author shall be liable for damages arising herefrom. If professional advice or other expert assistance is required, the services of a competent professional should be sought.

Library of Congress Cataloging-in-Publication Data is available

A catalogue record for this book is available from the British Library

ISBN 978-0-857-08561-0 (paperback)

ISBN 978-0-857-08560-3 (ebk)   ISBN 978-0-857-08559-7 (ebk)

Cover design by Revert to Type

Set in 10/13pt Sabon by Sparks Publishing Services Ltd (www.sparkspublishing.com)

Printed in Great Britain by TJ International Ltd, Padstow, Cornwall, UK

Dedicated to my parents, for always supporting my purpose.

Contents

....

Acknowledgements

....

This book is for everyone who helped me Create A Powerful Purpose For My Life. I could not have done this without you.

To my family: John, Karen, Noah, and Jessica, for supporting me long before I had an Escape Plan. Thank you all for Energizing My Dreams. I love you very much.

To Josh and Josh Birt Productions for always helping me Ruthlessly Evaluate My Current Position. To Craig for helping me Develop a Can-Do Mindset. And to Laura for helping me Set Short-Term Benchmarks when I'd rather be doing anything else.

To Matt H. and the rest of Team Bring: Clete, Nic, Matt D., and TC, for helping me break the 10,000-Hour Rule and Avoid Willpower Depletion. You are proof that once you've wrestled, everything else in life is easy.

To Team Cheeky, past, present, and future. Thank you for helping me Build Rome Around My Safety Net. To Garett, Lindsey, Aja, Matt G., and Michael for sharing your inspiring stories.

To all my Cheeky VIPs and Cheeky Champions. You are my best investments.

To my friends at ExCyte for helping me Think Inside the Box and Move Laterally. To my friends at Tree Star for helping me Manipulate Reality and see the world for the first time.

To Shaa for being an incredible friend and mentor. Thank you for your guidance.

To Jayson and my new MMT friends for all of your invaluable advice and for showing me how to Connect Without Getting Lost in the Crowd.

To Nils and Command + Z Content, and Ryan, Brent, and everyone at Story Ark for helping me take this book to the next level.

To Holly and everyone at Capstone for believing in this book and helping me bring it to life.

Foreword

It is such a privilege to be asked to write this foreword. Isaiah is a wonderful and rare person who not only wants to make a difference in this world, but is prepared to do whatever it takes to make that a reality. He is the living embodiment of this book.

I first came across Isaiah when he reached out to me on Twitter – I had just proudly published a photo of 50 Cent reading my last book, *Stop Talking, Start Doing*. In true Isaiah style, he tweeted me back – with a picture of himself reading my book whilst doing a handstand – along with a cheeky statement : "Bet he can't do this!" Now, I don't know whether 50 Cent can do that or not, but what I do know is that Isaiah got my attention and kept it. He created a relationship and put time and effort into building it. When I announced I was going to get all the big publishers together and run an event in London to teach other people how to create their own non-fiction bestseller, Isaiah was the first to book, even though he was living in Boston! Then, of course, he put everything he learnt into action and turned it into the wonderful and life changing book you find in your hands right now.

There are many books dedicated to finding our "purpose" in life, but none that lay out the benefits, consequences and crucially *how* you actually find that purpose as clearly as Isaiah does. This book demonstrates a strong correlation between being aligned with our purpose and living longer. So, yes, this really is a matter of life or death.

When I used to talk about "purpose" it conjured up images of yogis or social entrepreneurs who were changing the world. For sure, those people are likely to be more on purpose that the average Joe, but creating a powerful purpose and a fulfilled life is not something reserved for a particular "type" of person. It is available for everyone, as long as we make the conscious decision that that is how we want to live.

Once you are clear on what you want and crucially "why" you want it, your vision turns into a decision. So now it's your turn to get clear, to discover your why, to find your purpose and to take action.

Life is a journey and I want you to travel it well. Choose to be incredible.

Sháá Wasmund—Bestselling Author of *Stop Talking, Start Doing*

Preface

"*Man is condemned to be free; because once thrown into the world, he is responsible for everything he does. It is up to you to give [life] a meaning.*"

Jean-Paul Sartre

Growing up I spent my summers working on a sheep farm in the Pacific Northwest. I learned how to feed lambs, inject farm animals with anti-tick medication, build electrical fences, operate backhoes, drive tractors, and, of course, shear sheep. Once a year, usually in June, my boss would hire a shearer to visit the farm and shear over a hundred head of sheep in the same day.

You might imagine rounding up over a hundred animals and funneling them through a scary metal door toward a large man wielding an extremely loud and sharp buzzing device would be difficult. But, in reality, that isn't the case. Shearing sheep is pretty easy. This is because sheep aren't very smart. In fact, sheep are pretty stupid.

My job, on sheep shearing day, involved herding the sheep out of the pasture and into the large triangular cage. To do this, two or three other farmhands and I would circle behind the sheep, each of us holding two large sticks. We would position ourselves so that the sheep were between the triangular cage and us. Next, we would start banging the sticks together and walking towards the cage. Did I mention that sheep are terrified of everything, especially sticks?

The herd's reaction was always the same: one sheep would hear the banging sticks and take off running in the opposite direction, and immediately every other sheep would follow. The entire herd would run into the triangular pen. They did the work for us. All we had to do was keep banging the sticks and walking towards the gate.

Once the herd was inside, I would lure each sheep forward, inch by inch, with carrots and other treats. By the time a sheep was at the metal door, it was too late for it to escape. The sheep was cornered by the weight of the others. Its only option was to go through the door, where it would be pinned down and have its woolen fleece expertly removed. The shearing process wasn't painful—but still, the sheep hated it.

Sheep are the ultimate tacticians. They only respond to two things: sticks being banged behind them and carrots being held out in front of them. This is why it's so easy to shear sheep. Their herd mentality and lack of foresight make it very easy to funnel them down a narrow track until they are stuck; trapped by their own tactical nature. But sheep aren't the only animals that get stuck by groupthink and nearsightedness. It happens to humans too.

When we live our lives within the herd and without farsighted vision—like sheep instead of strategists—we end up trapped. Feeling trapped in a situation or bound by your circumstances is one of the worst feelings in the world. It can feel like you're slowly rotting while everyone else is getting ahead. The good news is that no matter how far down the tactical rabbit hole you have traveled, it's never too late to start thinking like a strategist. A strategist is someone who can see the end from the beginning and who acts independently from other people's expectations. A strategist is someone who maps out their purpose in life and works backwards to fulfill that purpose.

My life as a sheep

I was getting my PhD in Anatomy & Cell Biology at the University of Iowa when I realized I was stuck. I didn't want to be in school anymore. I had spent the last ten years chasing carrots and running from sticks, and had finally reached my dead end. I always wanted to be a doctor. But why? Had I just spent a decade chasing a shiny title?

Throughout high school and college, I chased awards and recognitions, like honor roll student, valedictorian, graduate, and PhD candidate. I followed a high-achieving path, doing the pre-med thing, volunteering at hospitals (because it looked good on applications), majoring in biology (because everyone else did), taking the MCAT, taking the GRE, getting my bachelors degree, applying to medical school, doing an internship, applying to graduate school, check, check, check, check. I checked every box I was supposed to without ever really asking myself where I was headed and why I was headed there.

Now, in my fifth year of graduate school, I realized I had never really given much thought to what PhDs did on a day-to-day basis either; I just liked the idea of being a doctor. My future was like a hazy dream, one that I only looked at for a few seconds every year. In the dream I was surrounded by money and beautiful women; peons beneath me called me "Doctor" and did my bidding (it was awesome). I didn't know exactly where I was going, but I knew one thing for sure: I would be happy when I got there.

Not so much. Getting a PhD is not what it used to be. PhD professors are 45% less likely to be tenured since the 1970s.[1] And if you are a recent PhD graduate or a postdoc, your chances of becoming a tenured professor drop to the single digits. Plus, life at large universities for most professors is miserable. They spend their time writing grant proposals and begging the government for money. Meanwhile, funding for big grants like R01 awards has dropped 18%.[2]

The Principal Investigator (PI) in my lab was one of these unhappy academics and we, his postdocs and graduate students, bore the brunt of his frustrations. While I was a student in his lab, he successfully fired or kicked out one postdoc, one technician, and two graduate students. He verbally abused both the technician and graduate students for months before they left. It was common to see his students crying in the back corners of the cafeteria lounge after meeting with him. The odd thing about academia is PhD professors are completely in control of their students' futures, yet they never receive any kind of management or interpersonal skills training.

I realized I did not want to be a professor. But I still didn't know what I wanted to be. More importantly, I didn't know *who* I wanted to be. As smart as I claimed to be, I never sat down to define a purpose for my life. As a result, I was stuck. I tried talking to my PI, who was also my advisor, about pursuing a career track outside of academia, but he didn't want anything to do with it. In graduate school, if at any time you decide you don't want to be a professor, you're labeled a failure. You instantly become the black sheep and, as a result, are quickly blacklisted.

Almost immediately my mentor started withdrawing his support. Worse still, my academic fate was entirely in his hands. To graduate with a PhD in the medical sciences you have to get the permission of a committee of five doctors. Every committee has a chair that has final say and, unfortunately, my committee chair was my PI. Though I had fulfilled all of the objective requirements, he determined I wasn't ready to move on. I could only wait to be released.

I tried everything to get out of graduate school. I put in more hours, I went to more seminars, I did more experiments, I read more articles, I wrote more, I networked more; but there was no escape. I even tried working less. No dice. I was stuck. Every hour of every day, I thought about quitting, but I couldn't stand the thought of throwing away the previous five years. Too miserable to move forward, too invested to turn around.

Eventually, stress started to take its toll. I remember sitting at my lab bench one afternoon when suddenly my pulse jacked up to 120 beats per minute and my face went white. I started sweating. I couldn't breathe. I didn't know what to do. Was I having a heart attack? Was I having a stroke? I ran to the emergency room, sprinted through the sliding doors, and yelled at the triage nurse, "I'm having a heart attack!" She replied calmly, "No you're not. Sit down and relax." I wasn't having a heart attack (I was only 29); I was having my first panic attack. As my anxiety prolonged, unabated, I experienced panic attacks almost daily.

A few months later, during a routine physical, my doctor found a large number of red blood cells in my urine. That's when things got weird. I was put through a battery of horrific tests including CAT scans with radioactive contrast dye, manual prostate evaluations, a kidney biopsy, and two (yes, two!) cystoscopy exams where a doctor slides a flexible camera the size of a #2 pencil up your urethra and into your bladder. How did I get here?

I developed a kidney disease brought on by stress-induced inflammation. I had hit rock bottom. I lived the next two months floating here and there through my life like a helium balloon slowly deflating. I was a copy of a copy of myself. I tried doing different things like going to meditation classes, joining book clubs, and even taking golf lessons. I knew I was missing something, but I didn't know what. These new things didn't fulfill me. I was still lost. I was still stuck.

From sheep to strategist

I was walking down the halls of MERF, the big green research building in Iowa City that I had been coming to for the last five years, when I noticed a flier posted to a bulletin board. The flier was promoting a seminar and, in the small print, it read, "Take responsibility for yourself." I stopped and stared at that flier for a very long time. In my head, I heard the words, "You're responsible for your own life" over and over again. A light went on. I was stuck in my own life because of my own actions. I was in graduate school by choice; the responsibility for my unhappiness was my own. Hearing this in my own head, reading it on the wall, and giving it a name really affected me. I was a sheep. I had spent the last ten years running away from sticks and chasing carrots. Instead of finding my own purpose and working to fulfill it, I had been working to fulfill other people's purposes. Everything turned around in that moment.

Over the next six months, I initiated a series of steps that helped me get out of graduate school, get my PhD, get healthy, get the job of my dreams, and position myself for continual growth, promotion, and success. I mastered the art of strategic thinking and—through a series of self-directed actions—continue to fulfill my overall purpose in life.

Within three years of graduating with my PhD, I successfully launched three multinational businesses, consulted for several Fortune 500 companies, coached over 50 professionals, managed an international multimillion dollar product line, gave over 250 seminars in 22 different countries, and published this book.

The notion that successful people are an elite class of well-connected individuals who have it all figured out and calmly carry out proven recipes for achievement and fulfillment is a misconception. Likewise, the idea that all successful people are lone wolves who fire their bosses and swim upstream is foolish. The truth is, your story won't fit into any specific mold. The starting point for success is knowing you will have to be supremely strategic in order to achieve your purpose. The key is taking responsibility for your own life and where it goes. The only person who can give your life meaning—the only person who can find your life's purpose—is you.

Introduction

"*I used to think that information was destroyed in black holes. ... This was my biggest blunder, or at least my biggest blunder in science.*"

Stephen Hawking

I've always been fascinated by black holes. The idea of some massive force so intense that absolutely everything is pulled into it is awe-inspiring. Nothing escapes a black hole. In fact, black holes are called "black" exactly because nothing escapes them—not even light. The world's top physicists used to believe that anything that entered a black hole was obliterated. But this is no longer a popular viewpoint. Current research shows that, instead of destroying objects, black holes *transform* them.

Imagine if your purpose in life was as powerful as a black hole. With a force this strong, absolutely everything in your life would be pulled towards it. Nothing would escape. Every thought, every action—your entire identity—would be sucked into it. And, as a result, who you are, what you have, and how you live would be completely transformed.

Determining your ultimate purpose in life is the toughest decision you will ever make, which is why so few people actively decide on one. Instead, most people let life make this critical decision for them. These people fritter their lives away in an endless stream of tiny, meaningless decisions that elicit no great change and leave no real impact. They spend all their time and resources putting out day-to-day fires and focusing on short-term objectives.

Black Hole Focus will show you how to avoid this hollow fate, how to decide your purpose, and how to align your life around your chosen path. It will show you how to determine your current position in life and how to change it. The first section discusses why you need to actively find a purpose for your life. The second section digs into the process of transforming your entire life so that it's completely aligned with your new purpose. The third section reveals how to fulfill your purpose in the face of adversity.

Each chapter is built around cutting-edge science in the fields of psychology, physiology, and motivational theory, as well as my own first-hand experiences and the experiences of other highly successful people. These include medical practitioners, research scientists, lawyers, corporate executives and small business owners. By reading this book, you will gain in-depth knowledge of what you really want in life and how to get it.

I am excited for you!

PART ONE

Why You Need a Purpose

"I would rather be ashes than dust! I would rather that my spark should burn out in a brilliant blaze than it should be stifled by dry-rot. I would rather be a superb meteor, every atom of me in magnificent glow, than a sleepy and permanent planet. The proper function of man is to live, not to exist. I shall not waste my days in trying to prolong them. I shall use my time."

Attributed to Jack London

1

Make Your Purpose a Matter of Life or Death

···

"Would it not be strange if a universe without purpose accidentally created humans who are so obsessed with purpose?"

Sir John Templeton

Purpose is a matter of life and death. Your purpose reflects your ability to derive meaning from your life's experiences, as well as your ability to make focused and intentional decisions.

Most people have faced circumstances that made them feel purposeless at one time or another. This point may have come after the freshness of a new job faded away or after the excitement of a new relationship wore off. Or it may have come after losing a job, experiencing the death of a family member, or being diagnosed with a serious illness. You feel empty and start questioning whether or not part of your life, or your entire life, has any meaning.

My last year in graduate school was absolutely miserable (see Preface). I couldn't grow. I couldn't move forward. It was like trying to run a car on a dead battery. You can't start. You can't turn over your engine and take any action. Instead, feelings of anger, fear, guilt, and sadness start to sink in. People who fail to regain their sense of purpose during these times eventually stop feeling anything. They enter a state of apathy, which is a breeding ground for illness and death.

Purpose linked to longevity

In *The Blue Zones*, Dan Buettner[1] describes regions of the world where people commonly live active lives past 100 years old. Buettner discusses a particular Blue Zone located on the northern part of the main island of Okinawa. He calls this place 'ground zero' for world longevity because people in this zone have the longest disability-free life expectancy in the world. These Okinawans live about seven good years longer than the average American. They

The more purpose you inject into your life, the brighter your internal spark will burn, the longer you will live, and the more productive you will be while you're alive.

also have one-fifth the rate of colon and breast cancer, and one-sixth the rate of cardiovascular disease. The Okinawan language has no word for "retirement." Instead, there is one word Okinawans live their life by: *ikigai*. Roughly translated, it means "the reason for which you wake up in the morning." Whether it's teaching karate at 102 or learning to fish at 104, the Okinawans maintain a strong sense of purpose. Buettner believes this intimate relationship with direction is why Okinawans often live so long.

The connection between birth and retirement

The two biggest risk factors in human mortality are birth and retirement. A study in the *British Medical Journal* followed a group of Shell Oil employees who retired at age 55 and another group who retired at age 65.[2] The study found the early retirees had a 37% higher risk of death than their counterparts.

That's not all. People who retire at 55 are 89% more likely to die in the ten years after retirement than those who retire at 65. Another study published in the journal *Archives of General Psychiatry* evaluated 246 people as part of the Rush Memory and Aging Project.[3,4,5] These people underwent cognitive and neurological testing once a year for ten years. Each person was asked to clearly define his or her purpose in life. After each participant's death, brain autopsies were performed. The researchers found that people who did not have a clear purpose in life had significantly faster rates of mental decline. (It is worth noting that no participants suffered from dementia.) These studies also linked not having a purpose in life to decreased longevity and a higher risk of Alzheimer's disease.

Your purpose—your *ikigai*—is fuel for your internal engine. It's what gives you direction and keeps you moving forward. The more purpose you inject into your life, the brighter your internal spark will burn, the longer you will live, and the more productive you will be while you're alive.

2

Make Your Purpose an Escape Plan

"What allows us, as human beings, to psychologically survive life on Earth, with all of its pain, drama, and challenges, is a sense of purpose and meaning."

Barbara de Angelis

In his book, *Awaken the Giant Within*, Anthony Robbins[6] drives home the point of living with a strong purpose in life, by telling the story of a man's harrowing escape from a Nazi prison camp.

Nazis stormed into Stanislavsky Lech's home, arrested him and his entire family, and sent them to a death camp in Krakow. Soon after, Lech's family was shot before his eyes and his son was murdered in a gas chamber. Forced to work as a laborer clearing dead bodies from the camp, Lech somehow continued living. It wasn't long before he looked at the horror around him and decided that he had to escape.

Escaping from the death camp became Lech's sole purpose in life, his obsession. Every thought, every step, every action revolved around answering the question, "How can I escape?" And he seemed to be the only one. Everyone else had given up. For weeks Lech asked the other prisoners, "How can we escape this horrible place?" The answers he received were always the same: "Don't be a fool, there is no escape," or "Don't torture yourself, just work hard and pray you survive." But Lech wouldn't accept it. One day, while being forced to clean the gas chambers, he saw a huge pile of bodies that had been shoveled into the back of a truck. This was his chance.

> ...finding a purpose for living is the only way to escape from a life of mediocrity and meaninglessness.

As the end of the day neared and the work party headed back into the barracks, Lech ducked behind the truck, ripped off his clothes, and dove naked into the pile of bodies. He remained completely still and pretended to be dead even as he was crushed by more and more bodies heaped on top of him. He was surrounded by the smell of rotting flesh and the rigid remains of other dead prisoners. After several torturous hours of waiting, Lech heard the truck's engine starting. Soon, the truck stopped and dumped its cargo into a giant open grave outside the camp. Lech remained there for many more hours until nightfall. Then, when he was sure no one was there, he climbed out of the mountain of dead bodies and ran naked 25 miles to freedom.

Even in unthinkable circumstances, as Ernest Hemingway famously wrote, "a man can be destroyed but not defeated."[7]

This story is wrenching and extreme, but its larger truth is important: finding a purpose for living is the only way to escape from a life of mediocrity and meaninglessness. Purpose saved Stanislavsky Lech. His sense of purpose, his burning desire to live, is the one thing that separated him from the other prisoners who shared his circumstances. Whether you find yourself held captive by your circumstances, your relationships, or your own emotions, you can take back control by harnessing the power of purposeful living.

3

Ask Why

"He who has a why to live can bear almost any how."

Friedrich Nietzsche

A strong WHY will show you HOW. The most important part of changing your life is knowing why you are changing it. Knowing why you want to accomplish a goal is more important than the goal itself. A strong WHY will support your efforts, giving you the stamina necessary to survive any attack and the creativity necessary to overcome any obstacle. Without a strong WHY, Stanislavsky Lech would not have survived. Without a strong WHY, your purpose won't survive.

WHY is your premise. WHY is the reason behind everything you do. When I was in graduate school I got stuck because I forgot why I entered it in the first place. Also, I didn't really know why I wanted to get out. Think about how many people stay in miserable jobs and miserable relationships because they don't have a strong enough reason to get out. They're miserable, but they don't really know why they're miserable. Sometimes the fix is as simple as remembering why you took the job, became friends, or fell in love. But sometimes the WHY you went in with isn't strong enough to keep you moving forward, and the only way to move forward is to find a better WHY.

Your worst pain is your strongest WHY

People only do things for two reasons: to avoid pain or to experience pleasure. Pain, in particular, is a very powerful motivator. Have you ever heard the phrase, "I hate to lose more than I like to win?" This is true for everyone: we hate pain more than we like pleasure. In fact, we are biologically driven to avoid pain over gaining pleasure.

The only way to fulfill a worthwhile purpose for your life is to focus on what is causing you pain, and then make a decision to never experience that pain again.

The amygdala is the fear response center of our brains. It uses two-thirds of its neurons searching for negativity. Once your amygdala finds negative information, it immediately transfers this information into your long-term memory. By contrast, positive experiences have to be held in awareness for more than twelve seconds in order for your brain to transfer them from your short-term to long-term memory banks.[8] This is why most people instantly forget praises, but can remember a single criticism for years. The key to changing your life is to use pain to your advantage.

Every rags-to-riches story is the result of pain and a strong reason to never experience it again:

- Oprah Winfrey, the media mogul and richest woman in the world, spent the first six years of her life living with her grandmother and wearing potato sacks as dresses. At the age of nine, she was sexually abused by two members of her family and a family friend. At the age of 14, she became pregnant, delivering a boy who died shortly after he was born.[9]

- Leonardo Del Vecchio is the owner of Luxottica, an eyewear molding company that makes brands like Ray-Ban and Oakley, and has 7,000 retail shops like Sunglass Hut and Lenscrafters. He grew up in an orphanage after his widowed mother could not afford to take care of him anymore.[10]

- Sam Walton, the founder of Wal-Mart, grew up on a farm in Oklahoma during the Great Depression. He worked slavish hours as a kid—milking cows, delivering papers, and selling magazine subscriptions to help his parents survive.[11]

- J.K. Rowling, before she started writing the Harry Potter series of books, was divorced and living on welfare with a dependent child. She is now worth more than $1 billion.[12]

Great success rarely exists without great pain. The only way to fulfill a worthwhile purpose for your life is to focus on what is causing you pain, and then make a decision to never experience that pain again. This decision is your WHY, and it is what will allow you to turn negativity into positivity. Start using the pain you've experienced, or the pain you're currently experiencing, to your advantage.

4

Know Your Needs

"The most basic of all human needs is the need to understand and be understood."

Ralph Nichols

Pain is the result of not having your needs met. Pain is your WHY—but why do you experience pain in the first place? People experience pain when they are not fulfilling their prime needs. Your prime needs are the desires that drive you to take action in your life; the things you want beyond your physical needs. All behavior is simply an attempt to meet your prime needs.

So, what are your prime needs? It turns out, in the universe of human needs there are three that sit at the top of the pyramid: growth, connection, and autonomy. Look at any number of books from renowned authors on this subject—Daniel Pink, Tony Robbins, Josh Kaufman, or Professors Lawrence and Nohria from Harvard—and their classifications of human needs all boil down to essentially the same things as well. If you're experiencing pain, it's because you're not meeting one or more of these prime needs.

Your pain may also be the result of your needs being off-balance or in competition with one another. For example, the need for connection and the need for autonomy often conflict. When your connection cup is overflowing—in romantic relationships, for instance—you may feel like you're suffocating or losing your identity. When your autonomy cup is overflowing, you may feel isolated and lonely. The only way to resolve the pain is to identify which needs are not being met and work to correct the deficiency. Once the painful experience is resolved, you can use it as a strong WHY—a reason to never experience that pain again.

...growth, connection, and autonomy... If you're experiencing pain, it's because you're not meeting one or more of these prime needs.

Growth is the master of your prime needs. Happiness is experiencing growth in every area of your life simultaneously, including growth in your levels of connection and autonomy. This book is about helping you find and fulfill a purpose that will supply you with continuous growth and high, balanced levels of connection and autonomy. But growth requires energy. Without energy, growth stops.

5

Energize Your Dreams

....

"Remember, Red, hope is a good thing—maybe the best of things—and no good thing ever dies."

Andy Dufresne in *The Shawshank Redemption*

The more you define your purpose, the more energy you'll have to achieve it. In high school, I hated sprints. The worst part of practicing any sport was the inevitable back-and-forth shuttle sprints that my coaches would make me do. Every day for football practice, in full gear, I would have to do 10×100-meter, 8×80-meter, 6×60-meter, and a variable number of 40-meter sprints. During wrestling practices I was forced to do an endless line of shuttle sprints down and back across the wrestling mat, or up and down a stairwell of stadium bleachers. I even had to do shuttle sprints, from base to base, during baseball practice.

Regardless of the sport, my coaches would never tell me how many sprints I had to do. Oh sure, they would tell me the number of sprints I was starting with, but never how many sprints in total. The number ALWAYS grew. "Not fast enough," they would say. "Get back on the line … Do it again … And again … And again." The interesting part was, no matter how many sprints I did, whenever my coaches called out, "Last one, give everything," I was able to run faster.

Purpose equals hope equals energy. Defining the path in front of you will give you the energy you need to complete it.

The hardest part of doing these sprints was not knowing how many I had left. How was I supposed to know how hard to try (or how much to hold back) if I didn't know how many I had to do? But that was the whole point—to learn that no matter how many sprints I just did, I could always do one more. Over time, my coaches trained me to hold back less and less during these sprinting sessions. Still, I was always surprised by how much energy I found in myself whenever they yelled out, "Last one, give everything." I could always run my last sprint much faster than my second-to-last sprint. Why?

Purpose provides energy and clarity

In the 1950s, Curt Paul Richter,[13,14] a Harvard graduate and Johns Hopkins scientist, did a series of experiments that tested how long rats could swim in high-sided buckets of circulating water before drowning. Dr Richter found that, under normal conditions, a rat could swim for an average of 15 minutes before giving up and sinking. However, if he rescued the rats just before drowning, dried them off and let them rest briefly, and then put them back into the same buckets of circulating water, the rats could swim an average of 60 hours. Yes, 60 hours. If a rat was temporarily saved, it would survive 240 times longer than if it was not temporarily saved. This makes no sense. How could these rats swim so much longer during the second session, especially just after swimming as long as possible to stay alive during the first session? Dr Richter concluded that the rats were able to swim longer because they were given hope. A better conclusion is that the rats were able to swim longer because they were given energy through hope. The rats had a clear picture of what being saved looked like, so they kept swimming.

The reason that I (or anyone) will feel a rush of energy close to the finish line of a sprint workout is the same reason rats swim longer after being saved; because the future is defined. Purpose equals hope equals energy. Defining the path in front of you will give you the energy you need to complete it. The key is to positively visualize the end at the beginning. You don't have to actually see the finish line; you just have to envision it. Vision creates hope, or a feeling of expectancy. And hope creates energy.

6

Start at the End

"What we call the beginning is often the end. And to make an end is to make a beginning. The end is where we start from."

T.S. Eliot

Naming your purpose in life is not an end in itself, but it is the beginning of getting what you want. In his book *Breaking In*,[15] Evan Farmer tells the story of Jim Carrey, the wildly successful comedian and actor. In 1987, Carrey was a struggling 25-year-old comedian, spending most of his time in his car and looking for odd jobs. One night, Carrey drove himself up into the Hollywood Hills and, sitting on Mulholland Drive, overlooking Los Angeles, wrote himself a check for $10 million. He dated the check for Thanksgiving 1995 and, in the memo, added, "For acting services rendered." Carrey kept the check in his wallet for seven years until, in 1994, he found out he was going to make $10 million for acting in the movie *Dumb and Dumber*.

All great stories are created in reverse order

A screenplay, or movie script, is an extremely stripped-down version of a story. But, like every good story, it has a purpose, or plot, that culminates in one climactic moment. Screenwriters are strategists. Professional screenwriters know the best way to write a script is to construct a plot by writing backwards from the climax, using reverse cause and effect.[16] The climax is the object of the plot and the point on the horizon that your story moves towards. For example, in the movie *Gladiator*, the object of the script is that Maximus (Russell Crowe) defeats the Emperor Commodus (Joaquin Phoenix) and with his dying words restores Marcus Aurelius' wishes, returning the power of Rome to the Senate. Working backwards from this climactic moment (the effect), you can string together a series of causes (Maximus' imprisonment, Marcus Aurelius' death, etc.) to create an

The only way to find and fulfill a worthy purpose is to name it and work in reverse order to achieve it.

Academy Award-winning movie. Good screenwriters construct the entire plot of a movie simply by asking themselves, "What is the cause of this effect?" over and over again. The answers to this question are what fill in the story. In the same way, you can work backwards to build your life around your climax, or the fulfillment of your overall purpose. In doing so, your long-term goal is always in your sights.

All great people are ordinary people with great purposes

The only way to become the person you want to be in life is to find your purpose and give it a name. Naming is power. Naming your desires imprints them on reality. Now, it's real. Now, it's in front of you. And the mind will naturally focus on whatever is in front of it.

Turning your purpose into a reality by naming it is not *The Secret*;[17] it's science. Studies from Dominican University[18] and Virginia Tech[19] show that people who write down their goals are 33% more likely to achieve them. These same studies show that people who write down their goals make nine times more money than people who don't. Yet 80% of Americans don't have goals. In other words, four out of five people in America do not have a defined purpose in life.

Successful people have a strong, well-defined sense of purpose. First, they realized they needed a purpose. Then, they defined an endpoint for their purpose and worked backwards to fulfill it. The only way to find and fulfill a worthy purpose is to name it and work in reverse order to achieve it. This is the exact opposite of what tacticians do. Tactical people let to-do lists guide their lives, as if having meetings and putting out fires will help them fulfill their master plans. Do not fall into this trap. Trickle-forward goal setting does not work. Running errands and answering emails is not a strategy. Instead of living like a tactician, be strategic and do what's necessary to carefully craft an entire campaign for your life.

The rest of this book will take you step by step through the process of learning what you want in life and exactly how to get it. I challenge you to read through each step carefully and to complete the associated personal exercises. These steps are backed by science and include case studies chronicling how successful people from different backgrounds took these steps to break free from sticking points and achieve their biggest goals. Mapping your purpose in life is an exciting experience. Remember, details generate drive. The more detailed your map, the more energy you'll have to traverse the actual territory. Let's get started.

Trickle-forward goal setting does not work.

Case Study

Garett Manion, PharmD

Garett Manion, PharmD grew up in a small home in rural Washington. Although the family didn't have much, his parents taught him the importance of a strong work ethic and a good education. At a young age, Garett decided to pursue a doctoral degree. He opted to follow in the footsteps of classmates he admired by going into pharmacy school. He liked the idea of being a doctor—and getting a nice paycheck.

To get into pharmacy school, Garett chased a series of short-term goals to help him graduate at the top of his class. He worked hard to successfully complete the pre-requisites for the Washington State University School of Pharmacy, one of the leading pharmacy programs in the United States.

After a grueling four years of pharmacy school and completing the requisite 60-week unpaid internship, he graduated, again, at the top of his class. It didn't take long before Garett was offered a six-figure contract with an international retail pharmacy as well as a five-figure signing bonus. Within a few months, Garett was promoted to pharmacy manager at the busiest and most profitable store in the district. Life was great. Garett was living the dream. Unfortunately, it was a pretty boring dream.

Garett's pharmacy life was uneventful. All he did was count pills all day. He felt like he didn't have a purpose in life. Although Garett accomplished all of his goals, this wasn't the dream he had envisioned. As a pharmacist, he wasn't providing the patient care and therapy he was trained for; he was very literally a bean counter and working to increase the company's profit margins.

Garett was a tactician. He spent his life focused on the short-term tasks in front of him, like chasing prerequisites, certifications, and other "carrots." He never took time to ask himself what a pharmacist's life actually looked like and whether the ideas and theories set forth in school about patient care and therapy would be implemented in his day-to-day career responsibilities. Instead, he plugged along from start to finish without ever looking at the finish line. He never asked, "Why do I want to be a pharmacist in the first place?"

As a result, he locked himself into a narrow career path that didn't offer much flexibility when it came to personal fulfillment and professional satisfaction.

PART TWO

How to Find Your Purpose

"It's lonely at the top. Ninety-nine percent of people in the world are convinced they are incapable of achieving great things, so they aim for the mediocre. The level of competition is thus fiercest for 'realistic' goals, paradoxically making them the most time- and energy-consuming … The fishing is best where the fewest go, and the collective insecurity of the world makes it easy for people to hit home runs while everyone else is aiming for base hits. There is just less competition for bigger goals … Unreasonable and unrealistic goals are easier to achieve for yet another reason. Having an unusually large goal is an adrenaline infusion that provides the endurance to overcome the inevitable trials and tribulations that go along with any goal. Realistic goals, goals restricted to the average ambition level, are uninspiring and will only fuel you through the first or second problem, at which point you throw in the towel."

Tim Ferriss

7

Ruthlessly Evaluate Your Current Position

"Accept everything about yourself—I mean everything. You are you and that is the beginning and the end—no apologies, no regrets."

Henry A. Kissinger

You can't get to a future position until you define your current position. In 1704, a Scottish sailor named Alexander Selkirk was marooned on a deserted island off the coast of Chile. Selkirk's ship was destroyed by the sea, leaving him with a rifle, a small knife, and some carpentry tools. After regaining some of his strength, Selkirk explored the interior of the island looking for supplies, but all he found were goats, feral cats, and large rats. Feeling hopeless, Selkirk returned to the shoreline and slept in a cave. After about a month of lying around and catching fish, he became severely depressed and ill. Selkirk drowned in his sorrows by imagining all of the things that could have happened differently in the days, weeks, and months before he was shipwrecked. He cursed the heavens for his bad luck and blamed the universe for being against him.

Then, one day, while Selkirk was lying sick in his cave, he looked out and saw sea lions invading the shoreline to mate. He was forced to move inland or be killed by the sea lions. With the last of his energy, Selkirk moved to the island's interior and began to explore the forest again. This time, however, he saw things in a different light. Instead of sulking, Selkirk started to evaluate his current position without regard to the past or his emotions. He instantly saw opportunity. First, remembering the carpentry tools he had, Selkirk built a series of huts out of the native woods. Next, by trial and error, he domesticated the feral cats, which provided him with companionship and protected him from the large rats. Finally, he

The only way to get to where you want to go is to ruthlessly evaluate where you are now. The key here is that your biggest obstacle in life is always yourself—not external factors.

taught himself to hunt the goats and made clothes out of their hides. Selkirk thrived on the island until his rescue many years later.

Define where you are and what you have, without prejudice, and you will be ready to fulfill your purpose in life. Selkirk's story is recounted by Robert Greene and 50 Cent in *The 50th Law*[1] and illustrates an important point: seeing your current position clearly is the first step to moving forward and making your life better. Regardless of what you want to accomplish, achieving your goal requires you to take careful stock of your assets and liabilities, as well as your strengths and limitations. The reason most people have a hard time explaining what they want in life is because they don't know what they already have. You can't move forward until you acknowledge where you're standing. Before you decide on a mission for your life, you must identify and name your current reality.

Eliminate the prejudice of your own perspective

The only way to define your current reality is to completely erase the past and disregard the pull of emotions from your mind. This step is more difficult than it seems. Every decision that you make during the day is colored by your past experiences and your emotions. Usually, this is a good thing, because it keeps you from repeating the same mistakes. However, in order to define where you are right now, in this exact moment, you must forget the past and treat your emotions as a disease. Any feelings—especially those of fear, anger, sadness, or guilt—will prevent you from objectively measuring your current station in life.

Once your mind is totally clear and in the present, imagine you were dropped from the sky into your current life as it stands right now. See your life from the viewpoint of an astronaut returning to the Earth after hundreds of years in outer space. How would a complete stranger describe your life right now, with no knowledge of past successes and failures, and no knowledge of your emotions and desires? Carefully measure your assets and liabilities, your strengths and your limitations, as well as those of your connections.

Complete this exercise from both a personal and a professional perspective. For example, if you are an award-winning chef, make a note of the cooking skills you have, as well as those you lack. However, ignore your past awards because they are of no use to you in the present.

Next, like Selkirk, find opportunity in your current situation. Where is there opportunity for personal and professional growth in your life right now, in this moment, with no regard to your past?

Judge past actions ruthlessly

Keep your emotions turned off but let your past come into play. What have you accomplished? What have you failed to accomplish? Ignore excuses or rationalizations that come into your head. Ignore your emotions and any attempts that your mind makes to justify what you are in the process of accomplishing. Refuse to evade reality by pretending things are one way when they are really another. Only then will you be able to see where you stand and how far you are from achieving your goal. Take careful notice of your victories and your defeats. Are there any patterns? What have you been particularly successful at? Do your failures have anything in common?

Own up to your current place in life

Now that you know where you stand, embrace it. Realize that only you are responsible for both the good and bad in your life. It is your own bad strategies—not God, the universe, or the unfair opponent—that are to blame for your failures. This mindset will free you from excuses and open your mind to the numerous possibilities existing in your life. Instead of getting defensive about past mistakes and failures, learn from them and search out new opportunities to face and similar challenges to surmount. Once you do this, you will start creating your own second chances.

The only way to get to where you want to go is to ruthlessly evaluate where you are now. The key here is that your biggest obstacle in life is always yourself—not external factors. Stop trying to change external factors and focus on changing yourself. Take complete responsibility for the person you are right now, including everything that you have or have not accomplished in life. Taking responsibility in this way will help you consolidate your current position in life with complete confidence and integrity. Once you know exactly where you are and who you are, you can strategically determine where you want to go and who you want to be.

8

Create a Wish List of Actions

"Do you want to know who you are? Don't ask. Act! Action will delineate and define you."

Thomas Jefferson

I had no idea what I wanted to do after getting my PhD. The best description I could muster for my future was "something else." My entire life had been geared towards working either with patients as a clinician or doing cancer research as a professor. As my last few years of graduate school unfolded, I realized that neither option was a good fit for me. All of the residents and young medical doctors I knew worked 80-hour weeks, running circles in the hospital with cheap cups of coffee attached to their lips. Likewise, all the post-docs and assistant professors I knew lived in 10-foot by 10-foot prison cells called labs, repeating experiments and writing grant proposals that failed to get funded 93% of the time. The worst part was that everyone was unhappy.

I needed to find a new name for my future. I spent 23 years in school to be a doctor and my future looked bleak. I started to entertain new options. The first question I asked was, "What am I qualified to do?" I made a list of the skills I acquired in the past, and skills I was currently using. Next, I tried to find a job in line with my qualifications. Here's what I came up with: post-doc, professor, clinician, and intellectual property lawyer. I actually considered the latter until I found out that I needed a law degree in addition to my PhD. I was not about to spend over $100,000[2] on another three years of school.

Making a wish list of actions, or writing down what you want to do on a daily basis, is the first step to defining your ultimate endpoint.

What did I want to do? Why couldn't I figure it out? The problem was that I was trying to work forward. I was trying to use the things

I had done in the past and the things I was currently doing to name my future. What I needed to do was name my future and adjust what I was doing to get there. Instead of focusing on my qualifications, I needed to focus on my aspirations and work backwards to align my qualifications.

Making a wish list of actions, or writing down what you want to do on a daily basis, is the first step to defining your ultimate endpoint. After failing to figure out my future by working forward, I started to work backward. I made a list of the things I wanted to be *doing* in my future. In other words, I made a wish list of *actions*: traveling the world, writing, teaching, consulting, starting a business, speaking in front of an audience, building professional relationships, pushing the cutting edge of technology, learning from a variety of scientific disciplines, and working from home or on the road. This list was my endpoint. It's where my purpose started.

9

Name Your Future Position

"But why, some say, the Moon? Why choose this as our goal? And they may well ask, why climb the highest mountain? Why, 35 years ago, fly the Atlantic? ... We choose to go to the Moon in this decade and do the other things, not because they are easy, but because they are hard, because that goal will serve to organize and measure the best of our energies and skills, because that challenge is one that we are willing to accept, one we are unwilling to postpone, and one which we intend to win."

John F. Kennedy

In graduate school, once I made my wish list of daily actions, I started searching for a position, or job title, that would allow me to consistently take those actions. Eventually, after several months of attending seminars and conferences, scouring the Internet, and reading industry articles, I came across the phrase *Application Scientist*. It fit perfectly. It checked all the boxes ... *my* boxes. Two weeks later, a privately held company offered me a position. The title: Application Scientist.

You can climb *any* mountain once you name its peak. The crew for Apollo 11 had been intensively training as a team for many months. The launch went off without a hitch. Once in space, Edwin (Buzz) Aldrin carefully navigated the Lunar Module to the surface of the moon. Buzz had to fly longer than planned, in order to avoid a field of boulders, and touched down on the moon with less than 40 seconds of fuel remaining. The Module landed at exactly 4:18 p.m. EDT on July 20, 1969. After six more hours of preparation, Commander Neil Armstrong exited the Module and became the first human to set foot on the moon.[3]

Forty-three years later, Felix Baumgartner, a 43-year-old Austrian man, jumped out of a ballooned capsule 128,000 feet above the earth. The capsule was raised into the stratosphere during the final manned flight for the Red Bull Stratos mission. Baumgartner fell to earth in a pressurized space suit that prevented him from being crushed as he broke the sound barrier and accelerated through the heavens at 833.9 miles per hour. He became the only man to achieve supersonic speed without a jet or space shuttle. In fact, Baumgartner set four different records, including the "highest manned balloon flight," "freefall from highest altitude," "supersonic speed in free-fall," and "longest freefall time."[4]

There are two beliefs you should live your life by. First, you can do anything you want in this life. Human beings have sent people to the Moon, eradicated deadly diseases, and connected the world with the Internet. Anything is possible. Second, life really is a journey, not a destination. Human beings are 5% matter and 95% constant will. And constant will, or constant desire, by definition, is never satisfied. No matter what you succeed in doing, you will want to succeed at doing something else afterwards. And if you don't, you'll retire and slowly die. Like the old Haitian proverb says: "Behind the mountains are more mountains."

Given these two beliefs, the best course of action is to choose a massive purpose and work your entire life to fulfill it. In other words, choose the tallest mountain peak you can fathom and start climbing. There's no mountain peak too tall and, even if you fail to reach the summit, the climb itself will fulfill you.

You must believe you can do anything

You can achieve greatness. No matter where you are in life right now, there is something you can be uniquely incredible at. But before you can be incredible, you must believe that you can do anything. That's the first step. The next step is a little harder: you must decide what you want to be incredible at.

Many online tests, career quizzes, and books have been created to help you find your purpose in life. The problem is that all of these methods and formulas are built for large groups of people. They have to be; no test can find the purpose for the seven billion people on Earth. This is why even the most exquisite purpose finder will try to fit you into one of two- or three-dozen categories. Instead, you need to fit yourself into one of seven billion categories. There is only one you; your purpose is different compared to everyone else's purpose, and—good news—you get to decide what that is!

Before deciding on your purpose, however, you need to set your mind right. Never set a goal when you are in a bad mood or when you're looking at life with a limited lens. If you're in a negative emotional state, do something to cheer yourself up. Listen to music, read something inspirational, go for a walk or run, talk to a friend, or dance around. Next, make sure that you've taken the limits off of your mind. Remember, anything is possible, and everything is waiting for you. Success is not a small well of water that's hard to find and on someone else's property. Success is a massive ocean that everyone has access to. All you have to do is grab your bucket and start scooping. Then, go back for more. And more. And more. It's an ocean—it never runs out. This is called having an *abundance mentality*. Once you are in a positive, upbeat mood, and once you're open to seeing all the abundant possibilities for your life, get a pen and pad of paper (or your laptop or tablet) and find somewhere to sit down and write.

With your attitude adjusted and your pen in hand, start writing down everything you want to own, everything you want to do, and everything you want to be. Write down BIG things, not something on your daily to-do list or yearly calendar. For example, you could write, "Own a profitable business," "Create a top-selling product," "Be CEO of a Fortune 500 company," "Be paid to speak in front of 10,000 people," "Write a *New York Times* bestseller," "Manage a nonprofit organization that changes the world," "Be married with four kids," or "Build a house on the ocean."

Focus on things that involve creating something or being someone special; these are the kinds of desires that are worth spending your entire life pursuing. This is your mountain peak, your purpose in life. As you write, think of who you want to be five to ten years from now. Don't try to see *how* you will get there; just focus on *what* you want and *who* you want to be. Your goal is to find your mountain peak, not the hiking path you will be using to scale the mountain.

Understand that finding your purpose requires you to name your future position in advance.

Don't be specific. Your goal is to name your purpose in life, not describe it. In fact, you shouldn't be close enough to your mountain peak to describe the terrain on the summit. Write BIG and write without limits. Don't be afraid of writing down something too big; you can always change your purpose down the road. Often, the thing you fear writing the most is the thing you want the most.

The best way to name your position, to define your purpose in life, is to question your current actions and pay attention to your emotions. As you're writing, ask yourself these key questions: what do I currently enjoy doing? What do I lose myself in while I'm doing it? What do I do in my free time? Chances are, you're probably already spending time doing things that are naturally in line with your purpose.

Finally, as you're brainstorming, pay close attention to your feelings. Is there something that makes you leap on the inside? Is there something that instantly fills you with an intense emotion, no matter what it is? What is the one thing you wrote that broke your heart and almost made you want to cry because you were suddenly filled with a powerful sense of yearning? What is the one thing you wrote that made you instantly feel afraid or insecure? What is the one thing you wrote that made you angry at someone else for already having it?

Keep writing until something makes you come alive on the inside. Then give it a name, say it out loud, write it out in big bold letters, and put it on your wall. Understand that finding your purpose requires you to name your future position in advance. And there is a very real possibility that you can do virtually anything—not alone, and not without new information—if you really decide to do it. Everything is within your ultimate grasp.

Case Study

Garett Manion, PharmD

After three years of working as a retail pharmacist, Garett decided to make a change. He realized the only way to move forward was to define his current position, pick a future position, and work in reverse order to connect the two. First, Garett took stock of his life. He carefully considered his strengths and weaknesses, as well as his assets and liabilities.

Garett then realized one of his key strengths was teaching. He loved helping people learn, and he was good at it, which is why he was promoted to manager so quickly at the retail pharmacy he worked for. Garett also realized that, while he had plenty of money, he lacked outlets for professional growth. This was a major liability. However, he had numerous connections at the Washington State University School of Pharmacy. In fact, he had trained several university students at the pharmacies he managed. After identifying his current position, Garett's next step was to evaluate and determine his ideal future. After several days of deliberation, Garett decided he wanted to:

- *Talk more with patients*
- *Interact with colleagues*
- *Teach*
- *Publish journal articles*
- *Help push the field of pharmacy forward*
- *Spend time outside.*

Creating this wish list of actions had a dramatic effect on Garett's perspective. His true purpose came forcefully into focus. He recognized that although he wanted to continue his current professional pursuits, his purpose was to teach. The next step was to give this purpose a name.

Shortly after finishing his wish list of actions, Garett wrote down the words, "Professor of Pharmacy." It was a moment of reckoning. In retrospect, it was completely obvious. He was meant to be a professor. He just never thought about it in the right way. Garett made a few calls to some colleagues at the Washington State University School of Pharmacy and two months later he was hired as an adjunct professor. The great part is that Garett did not have to give up his current position, or anything else for that matter, to find his true purpose and move towards it. (See Chapter 31 for more on getting what you want without giving up anything in return.)

Garett is currently an adjunct faculty member who is excited about advancing his new career. But this time, instead of chasing each successive goal with his head down, he is pulled forward by his endpoint. He is completely focused on his finish line.

10

Determine Your Core Priorities

"Things which matter most must never be at the mercy of things which matter least."

Johann Wolfgang von Goethe

As a strategist, you must first find and name your overall purpose in life. Identify what makes you come alive and leap on the inside. Find a goal that pulls you towards it just by saying its name. Then, identify the core priorities presently guiding your life. Your priorities are the values and the traits you give a lot of importance to; things you perceive as ethically good.

Examples of core priorities many people have include freedom, security, love, connection, intimacy, health, success, significance, vitality, cheerfulness, productivity, graciousness, contribution, wealth, patience, piety, faith, intelligence, and wisdom. These core priorities are different for everyone. The key is that your priorities are what got you where you are today—for better or worse—and they will get you where you want to go tomorrow.

In physics, a singularity is a point of infinite density and infinitesimal volume. Singularities exist at the center of black holes, which are regions of space that have a gravitational field so intense that no matter or radiation can escape.[5] Likewise, the pull of your purpose combined with your core priorities is so intense, so massive, that nothing you do can escape its influence.

Combined with a strong purpose, your core priorities have irresistible force over your life.

Every thought you have, every decision you make, and every action you take is pulled by this force. The problem is that most people never actively name or change the priorities guiding their lives. As a result, they have no idea why they do the things they do. By naming your core priorities, you will see *why* you do the things that you do. You will also discover *how* you will need to change your core priorities in order to achieve your biggest goals.

Make a list of all the things you currently value

To determine your core priorities, make a list of all the things you currently value. Start by writing down all of your strengths:

- Do you value your freedom?

- Do you value your security?

- Do you value your graciousness, your cheerfulness, your intelligence, or your vitality?

Focus on the strengths that have helped you accomplish goals in the past:

- Which strengths are you proud of?

- Which of your positive traits have helped get you to where you are today?

- Is it your drive to be important or to be significant?

- Is it your desire to contribute something and leave a legacy?

- Is it your desire for more freedom, more wealth, or more health?

Consider the inspiring traits that you see in other people:

- Which traits do you admire in others?

- Which traits do you desire?

These are the core priorities guiding your life.

The relationship between your life's purpose and core priorities is the same as the relationship between job title and job qualifications. Your core priorities qualify you for your purpose. And just as you can adapt or add to your qualifications to make yourself a better candidate for a job, you can adapt or add to your priorities to make yourself a better candidate for fulfilling your purpose.

In graduate school, after I identified the job title *Application Scientist*, I identified the best qualifications for fulfilling an Application Scientist's job requirements. Some of these qualifications, such as software development, were brand new. Others, such as public speaking, simply needed to be refreshed and brought to the forefront of my skillset. Aligning my qualifications was easy once I knew the name of the position I wanted.

Similarly, you can change your priorities to better qualify you for any new position you want to attain in life. Combined with a strong purpose, your core priorities have irresistible force over your life. This is the power of focus. If you're currently working as a bartender and want to be a famous comedian, you better add humor and connection to your list of priorities, or bump them up to the top of the list. By turning your attention to the skillset you need to achieve your purpose, your entire life will rearrange itself to foster that purpose.

11

Define Your New Core Priorities

"Just as your car runs more smoothly and requires less energy to go faster and farther when the wheels are in perfect alignment, you perform better when your thoughts, feelings, emotions, goals, and priorities are in balance."

Brian Tracy

Change your priorities and yovu will change your life. Your core priorities are the center blocks of your life.

Imagine your life is one giant Rubik's cube. In order to experience ultimate achievement and fulfillment, you have to reorder and align the cube's colored blocks. Any Rubik's cube connoisseur will tell you the most efficient and effective way to solve this puzzle is to set one block of any color in the center of one side of the cube and keep it there. This is your focal point. From this point, your goal is to manipulate and reorder that same side of the cube until every block matches the color of the block you set in the center. To solve the puzzle, repeat this sequence for all six sides of the cube.[6] Similarly, centering your core priorities is the essential step to aligning all the blocks of your life. The only difference is that your blocks will align themselves *automatically* once your core priorities are set.

Don't be afraid to let go of your old priorities

In the previous chapter, I showed you how to determine the core priorities currently guiding your life. These priorities are what got you to where you are today. They are exactly what you needed to achieve your goals in the past. However, your current priorities, by themselves, will not get you to where you want to go in the future. In order to achieve a new goal and fulfill your new purpose in life, you will need to change your priorities.

Most people have been guided by the same core priorities for years. They are so attached to their current priorities that to change even one of them would be like cutting off a body part. Some people identify so strongly with their current priorities, they knowingly sacrifice their biggest goals to avoid dealing with the temporary pain of change.

A few years ago, I went through the process of determining the top six core priorities that were guiding my life. After a lot of self-reflection, which included digging into the strengths I valued in myself and in others, I made the following list:

1 Independence

2 Vitality

3 Success

4 Toughness

5 Recognition

6 Image.

Putting my priorities down on paper was not easy. In fact, it was painful. I didn't like some of the items on my list and I was embarrassed by others. But I was determined to be completely honest with myself. I cannot begin to describe the level of clarity and insight I achieved by making this list. Suddenly, I was able to see why I did the things that I did. I finally understood the drivers behind the decisions and actions that shaped my life.

First, it was obvious that I placed a high level of importance on *independence*. This priority served me well during my high school and college years, as well as during my time in graduate school; both of these periods required extraordinary amounts of self-reliance and self-initiative. However, I had begun to rely only on myself to get things done. I would often find myself trying to control everything in my life in the hope of gaining more independence and freedom. Of course, this had the opposite effect and led to me being less free. If I wanted to achieve my new goals of being successful in business and entrepreneurship, I would have to replace this priority with something that valued connection, relationships, and trust.

I also came to the conclusion that it was time to re-place *toughness* with a new priority. For a long time I considered my ability to be tough, or my ability not to let my emotions influence me, to be one of my biggest strengths. This served me well when I left all of my family and friends in Spokane, Washington, to attend college 3,000 miles away in Pennsylvania. It also served me well as a scientist in graduate school.

You are in control of your priorities—you can erase old priorities and define new priorities at will.

However, this core priority was starting to close me off from oppor-tunities and other people. Trying to be tough would also lead me to engage in unnecessary and irrelevant conflicts. In order to fulfill my new purpose, I would have to start valuing openness, vulnerability, and authenticity.

Three of the priorities on my old list added energy to one another and became a very powerful force in my life. My desire for *success*, *recognition*, and *image* had dominated the majority of my decisions and actions. Every day, all day, I asked, "How can I get ahead?" This question served me my entire life and is what took me from rural Idaho (where I grew up) to getting my doctorate and traveling the world. I had an insatiable drive to grow in my finances, in my education, in my social status, and in my personal development. Unfortunately, there were times when I failed to rein in these desires, becoming too obsessed with achieving success, getting approval, and looking good. I also failed to define exactly what success looked like for me. I came to the conclusion that I needed better achievement-oriented priorities. I needed priorities that would focus on adding value to the world and leaving a legacy. On top of this, I needed priorities that would promote self-awareness and foresight.

Adding new priorities

My long-held priorities were what got me to my current position, but they were not going to get me to my future position. The first and most important priority that I added to my new list was *presence*. Without presence of mind, self-awareness, and being able to be present in the moment, I would not be able to enjoy any of my pursuits. I would also not be able to see all of the opportunities around me. Second, I added both *openness* and *relationships* to my list. If I wanted to be an effective author, I would have to learn to be uncomfortably vulnerable, transparent, and authentic. This openness would help me connect with other people, including my audience, fans, and readers. By valuing relationships, I would stay focused on building lasting connections that would add meaning to my life and the lives of others.

Then I added *contribution* to the list, which would help me redefine success and achievement. With contribution as one of my core priorities, I would stop asking, "How can I get ahead?" and start asking, "How can I add value?" Focusing on contribution would help me stay focused on building, creating, giving, and leaving a legacy.

Lastly, I added *strategy* to my list. Strategy meant staying focused on my long-term goal. I would be a strategist consumed with purpose rather than a tactician consumed with instant gratification. Valuing foresight in this way would prevent me from wasting my time. It would also encourage me to be more intelligent, patient, and wise. Most importantly, I would stop engaging in battles that did not matter. My new list of core priorities looks like this:

1 Presence

2 Vitality

3 Openness

4 Relationships

5 Contribution

6 Strategy.

While many of my priorities changed, *vitality* stayed exactly the same. I firmly believe that vitality should be near the top of everyone's list. Your new purpose may be important, but it's useless if you are unhealthy, sick, or dead. Of course, you can leave a legacy from the grave, but while you're here on Earth, the healthier you are, the more effective you are.

You never lose your strengths. Finding and fulfilling your purpose requires you to define your core priorities and develop new ones. There is no loss; you are merely adding to your repertoire. You are in control of your priorities—you can erase old priorities and define new priorities at will. The key is to define your new priorities with words that inspire you. Choose words that fill you with hope and energy, and drastically impact your decisions and actions. In this way, you will align your current life with your new purpose and guard yourself against distracting activities and emotions.

12

Set Short-Term Benchmarks

"People with goals succeed because they know where they're going."

Earl Nightingale

Objectives highlight your priorities. Without short-term benchmarks, the core priorities you just created will lose their luster. Most importantly, any momentum built towards aligning your life with your priorities will fade.

The best way to prevent this is to attach one aggressive goal to each of your core priorities. The key is to make each goal exciting and immediately actionable. If the goal doesn't get your mind racing and fill you with enthusiasm, drop it. If the timeline you set for the objective doesn't fill you with a sense of urgency and mild panic, shorten it. (I recommend staying within the one- to six-month range.)

For example, my second core priority is vitality. Previous objectives I've attached to it include "Join a Crossfit[7] gym tomorrow and attend two classes a week for three months" and "Build a complete home gym by the end of the month." For contribution, previous objectives included "Write two blog articles a week for the next six months" and "Donate $1,000 by February to a high school wrestling program."

Short-term benchmarks empower your priorities.

Here are my current core priority benchmarks (at the time of writing this book):

1 **Presence:** Meditate and pray for 20 minutes at the end of each day for the next three months.

2 **Vitality:** Join a Crossfit gym and go two days a week for the next nine months.

3 **Openness:** Tell one personal story in each blog post for the next three months.

4 **Relationships:** Develop 30 new close relationships with my readers over the next six months.

5 **Contribution:** Publish *Black Hole Focus* by this time next year (12 months).

6 **Strategy:** Launch the Cheeky Scientist® website by this time next month.

As soon as you hit one benchmark, create another. Eventually, you will have fashioned together a string of short-term targets. This string will auto-align your actions with your priorities, generating momentum towards your purpose in life. Short-term benchmarks empower your priorities. To supercharge your priorities, back them up with both a short-term benchmark and a strong reason WHY (see Chapter 3). For example, I would back up my second core priority, vitality, with the above benchmark and the following WHY: to stay out of the hospital and never again to feel as sick as I did in graduate school.

Case Study

Aja Davis, MS, MBA

Aja Davis loves science. She spent the majority of her time at Grinnell College taking science classes and working late afternoons in various laboratories. In 2004, she was accepted into the University of Iowa Pathology Masters of Science program. During her first year at Iowa, Aja was at the top of her class and settling into a new lab that studied natural killer cells (a cell type critical to warding off cancer).

Life was good. Aja had always wanted to be a professor and to help students reach their potential. She wanted to run a lab and publish papers and teach. But, a year into her Master's program, she realized that she wanted more—she wanted a career that not only fit her professional goals but also allowed her room to breathe. And she didn't want to have to rely on government funding to reach those aspirations. The National Institutes of Health budget was extremely low, severely limiting the number of approved grants each year. No grant, no lab. Hundreds of labs across the country were shutting down, including labs at the University of Iowa.

Aja was tired of an environment that relied on, as she put it, "leftovers." She didn't want her success to rest on how well she could beg for money. The more Aja thought about her future, the more she saw herself as a manager, or even as a successful executive at a scientific company. In 2007, she had a name for her new purpose in life: "MBA graduate and Fortune 500 executive team member." Her new goal would be to get her Master of Business Administration (MBA) degree and then get hired by a top-tier biotechnology or biopharmaceutical company. The only problem: Aja had absolutely no business experience. Aja knew the MBA would add a critical skillset to her toolbox, but also knew that she would have to evaluate her core priorities and align them with her new purpose. The first step was identifying the priorities currently guiding her life. These were the priorities she identified:

1. *Significance*

2. *Comfort*

3. *Intelligence*

4. *Friendliness*

5. *Individuality*

6. *Knowledge.*

Looking at this list, Aja knew she would have to make drastic changes in order to fulfill her new purpose. She would have to stop being concerned with significance. Aja always wanted to be "important;" while this can be a healthy desire, it sometimes led her to focus on what other people thought of her. If Aja was going to leave academia for business—or "sell out" as her peers called it—she would have to stop caring what other people thought. Instead, she would have to focus on being a leader, especially if she wanted to work her way into a management position. She would also have to stop caring about feeling comfortable. Changing career paths comes with a significant degree of discomfort. She might even have to get a little competitive and—yikes!—unfriendly.

Academia can be passive. During lab meetings, seminars, and classes, most people sit back and let others talk (or, not talk). There's an air of altruism that keeps people from being openly hostile or competitive, and allows their opinions to be heard and acknowledged. This was definitely not the case in the business world. Finally, while Aja kept intelligence as a priority, she learned to be more team-oriented. And she started to value results and effectiveness, or application, over pure knowledge. After a couple of weeks, Aja made a list of her new priorities:

1. *Leadership*

2. *Intelligence*

3. *Vulnerability*

4. *Strategy*

5. *Synergy*

6. *Effectiveness.*

These new priorities would help Aja fulfill her purpose of gaining an MBA and becoming a Fortune 500 executive team member. Above all, valuing leadership would help her dive into unknown waters and make a name for herself, as well as keep her on track for a career in management. Aja decided to bump intelligence up a notch because navigating her MBA program and the subsequent corporate maze would require a lot of smart, critical decisions. It would also require strategy, which she also added to her new list.

Aja added vulnerability so she would remember to face her fears and push past her comfort zone during the transition from academia to business. Since she lacked business training, she had to prepare herself to make mistakes and to learn quickly from them. She liked the idea of adding synergy to her list because it seemed like a good mix of individuality and teamwork. Synergy implied Aja could be her own person while communicating and working well with others. She replaced knowledge with effectiveness to encourage herself to apply what she learned. Academia involved learning for the sake of learning; in business, Aja would need to translate knowledge into action as quickly and productively as possible.

In 2007, after naming her purpose and rewriting her priorities, Aja was accepted into the University of Virginia Darden School of Business, one of the top business schools[8] in the United States. Two years later, Aja graduated from Darden and took a lucrative position as a sales and marketing manager at Amgen, a Fortune 500[9] biopharmaceutical company.

13

Tell Yourself an Inspiring Story

"A human being is nothing but a story with skin around it."

Fred Allen

What stories have you been telling yourself? The story of "I'm too young," "I'm too old," "I'm uneducated," or "I don't have enough experience"? You will live whatever story you tell yourself, so make sure you're telling yourself an inspiring one. Stories express meaning stronger than logical arguments and lawful formulations. Stories are the vehicles people use to give meaning to their experiences. And how you give meaning to or interpret your experiences will direct your life. No matter what you set out to do, achieving your goal will require stories. The key is to create positive and productive stories in line with your new direction in life. Your aim is to align your story with your priorities and purpose.

When I started speaking publically, I was extremely nervous. Before going on stage, my heart would begin to pound in my chest and I would start to sweat and get lightheaded from breathing irregularly. Sometimes I would have to go to the bathroom and do jumping jacks or wall pushups. This helped me stop consciously thinking about each breath and gave me an outlet for my nervous energy. It didn't help the sweating though. Five minutes before starting, I would splash cold water on my face over and over in an effort to calm down.

Eventually, I realized my body was not the problem. The problem was in my head. I was telling myself a bad story. I had recently started a new career in a field in which I did not have a lot of experience. Yet my main job was to teach other doctors about this field. I gave meaning to these facts by telling myself the following story: "You don't have enough experience. You're not qualified for this job. Who do you think you're fooling? If you mess up or don't know the

> **You will never fulfill a good purpose by living a bad story.**

Not only can you program your mind with a story—you can program someone else's mind.

answer to something, you will be exposed. It's only a matter of time before everyone knows you're a phony."

Of course I was nervous. How could anyone living this story not be terrified of speaking? I was telling myself a story of fear and failure. Having little experience and starting a new job were facts. Not having *enough* experience and not being qualified were my interpretations of the facts. Likewise, the possibility of not knowing the answer to a question was a fact, but being exposed as a phony for it was my interpretation. Together, these negative interpretations created a negative story—and I was the main character.

You will never fulfill a good purpose by living a bad story. Eventually, I recognized the bad stories playing in my head and decided to create a new story: "You are new and fresh to this field, which means you have more enthusiasm and can think outside the box more easily. Every question you don't know the answer to is a chance to learn and enhance your expertise. You are already successful in this situation."

Program your mind with positive storytelling

Storytelling is the oldest method of communication. Stories are used to record historical facts, educate people, express beliefs, set standards, and share experiences. Research on the human brain has shown it is predisposed to think in the terms of a story.[10] This predisposition is continuously reinforced and strengthened throughout the life of your brain. Imaging studies have shown that only a small, quarter-sized region of your brain lights up when someone tells you a series of facts. However, when someone tells you a story laced with those facts, or those facts in action, your entire brain lights up.

Not only can you program your mind with a story—you can program someone else's mind. A study at Princeton University found that when two people communicate through storytelling, neural activity becomes almost synchronous: the listener's brain activity mirrors that of the speaker's brain with a one-second lag.[11] Another study from the University of Missouri has shown that storytelling improves communication skills and prevents disease progression in patients with Alzheimer's and other forms of dementia.[12]

Storytelling is also used as a form of psychotherapy called *narrative therapy*.[13] It's based on narrative psychology, a viewpoint asserting that human beings shape their lives with stories. Narrative therapists work with their patients to develop better stories. In this process, a narrative therapist asks a patient questions to generate vivid descriptions of the patient's life events. The key is that the therapist will only ask questions that prompt positive descriptions not currently included in the plot of the patient's problematic story. This process helps people increase happiness and improve self-confidence by giving them happier, more empowering stories to live out. Narrative therapy has been shown to effectively treat a variety of psychological disorders, including major depression[14] and anorexia.[15]

Recognize the stories you tell yourself

The story of your life is made up of many little stories. First, you have an experience. Second, you interpret that experience, either subconsciously or consciously, thereby giving it meaning and turning it into a little story. Third, you take that little story and fit it into the big story of your life.

In order to change your big story, you have to change the little ones. The best way to do this is to increase your self-awareness and be on guard against negative scripts. For example, if someone doesn't smile back at you, you might be tempted to think, "They don't like me." That is a story. The truth is, you have no idea why that person didn't smile. Maybe they didn't see you, or maybe they have a headache or didn't sleep well. Similarly, if someone cuts you off in traffic, don't tell yourself, "They're a jerk" or "The Universe hates me." Those are stories. Recognizing the small stories you tell yourself will help you recognize the big stories you've been telling yourself for years. Live the story of fulfilling your purpose, not the story of failing.

14

Be the Hero of Your Story

....

"Imagination and fiction make up more than three-quarters of our real life."

Simone Weil

If your life were a movie, what would be the synopsis? Young athletes, especially those involved in individual sports, love *Rocky* movies.[16] In junior high and high school, my wrestling friends and I were constantly watching *Rocky* movies. We would watch a *Rocky* movie before practice, listen to the *Rocky* soundtrack during practice, and then watch another *Rocky* movie after practice. One of the most motivating moments of my life occurred during a *Rocky* movie.

The summer before my senior year of high school, I packed my bags and went to the University of Southern Oregon for my first J. Robinson Intensive Wrestling Camp.[17] This camp is rumored to have been on David Letterman's top ten list of places not to send your kids. The camp is designed to be a marine boot camp for wrestlers, and includes four or more excruciating workouts a day, crazed NCAA All-American counselors breathing down your neck, and no access to the outside world. But every Thursday, before lights out at night, we were allowed to watch a movie. More than 300 high school wrestlers would pack into a university classroom meant for 50 people and sit in front of an old-school TV/VCR setup. The last Thursday of camp, J. Robinson himself walked into the classroom and put in *Rocky II*.

The plot is simple: after losing to Apollo Creed in *Rocky*, Rocky Balboa tries to make money without boxing. Rocky's wife, Adrian, is pregnant, and doesn't want Rocky to box anymore because she is afraid he will get permanently injured. Rocky tries to make commercials endorsing different products but fails because he can't read. He tries to get an office job but fails because he doesn't have a degree. Eventually, he is forced to work as a manual laborer in a meat factory. As Rocky's life is falling apart, Apollo Creed is ridiculing Rocky and trying to bait him into a rematch. This sequence spans over two-thirds of the movie. Then, in the third act, Adrian becomes ill during the last months of her pregnancy and slips into a coma. When she finally wakes up, she pulls Rocky close, smiles, and says, "Win." Boom. Bells ring, the *Rocky* montage starts playing in the background, and the rest of the movie shows Rocky training for and winning his rematch against Apollo. Back in the classroom at J. Robinson, 300 wrestlers were calmly watching Rocky wimp out. But when Adrian said, "Win," and the *Rocky* music started playing, everyone went nuts. We all jumped up and started cheering and shouting. The next morning, we were put through the hardest workout of the entire camp, but it felt like nothing.

Achieve your biggest goals in life by being the hero of your story, not the spectator, loser, or victim. Stories are incredibly powerful. They have the power to define and influence you. They can create or destroy your future. If you want to fulfill your purpose in life, you have to make sure you identify yourself as the hero. As Rocky struggled to build a life outside the ring, he became the grunt of his own small stories—I'm a loser, I'm not smart, etc.—and his big story followed suit. "Win" changed everything. Rocky was empowered by thinking of himself as a fighter again and his small stories shifted from failure to inspiration. He found his purpose, his course was set in the right direction, his strengths were in alignment, and his drive and focus were locked. Our hero could be a hero again. It's impossible to watch that scene without being motivated by it.

Achieve your biggest goals in life by being the hero of your story, not the spectator, loser, or victim. Instead of seeing yourself as a grunt struggling uphill against the world, start seeing yourself as an adventurer, teacher, and connector of ideas and people. Actively choose the stories influencing your life and be the hero.

Know when to change your story

Why do epics such as *300*, *Joan of Arc*, *Braveheart*, and *Gladiator* continue to be popular?[18] It's because they all tell the story of one person, or a small band of people, alone in their struggle and fighting to the death against unthinkable odds. Think about it: being alone, or misunderstood, or against the world, is one of the most popular stories people play out in their heads. We identify so strongly with the few-versus-many narrative that this type of movie will be successful until the end of time.

Of course, there's nothing wrong with watching and enjoying these stories, as long as you are aware of their influence and their limitations. What part of these stories are you identifying with? The inspiring purpose and ultimate legacy of the hero, or his difficult circumstances? The story of your life shouldn't be one of constant lack and struggle against a cruel world until you're stabbed in the Coliseum. Be aware of what stories you identify with and how they may be influencing your own. If your story is not inspiring you, it's time to change it.

If your story is not inspiring you, it's time to change it.

15

Re-Write Your Story

"You must have control of the authorship of your own destiny. The pen that writes your life story must be held in your own hand."

Irene C. Kassorla

Seize the pen. It's time to get real. It's time to write a new story for your life. This story will be something that generations of people will read and be inspired by. This story will be bold, strong, and meaningful. This is your story.

Before you begin, find a place where you can be completely alone. You need to be alone so you are not influenced by any feelings of guilt, insecurity, or embarrassment. Realize other people's expectations can limit you mentally, even from a distance. When you are ready, start reflecting on the times in your life when you felt the most inspired.

When did you feel maximally empowered? What were you watching, reading, or doing? Was it a certain movie or part of a movie, a particular book or an excerpt from a book, an article, a painting, a picture, a quote, a website, a sermon, a speech, a performance, an activity, or a conversation? From memory, create a giant list of all the things that really inspire you. Don't Google anything and don't worry about your spelling.

Here is the list I made in 2010 when I was trying to change my story from Isaiah the struggling graduate student to Isaiah the successful author and entrepreneur:

- "It is better to live one day as a lion than 100 years as a sheep." — Italian proverb
- Individuality, one against the world
- San Giorgio Maggiore at Dusk by Monet
- Ayn Rand's West Point Graduation speech
- The end of the movie Rudy when his friend yells "who's the wild man now"
- High school wrestlers training to win a State championship, individual sports
- The Fountainhead, Zen and the Art of Motorcycle Maintenance, Assault on Lake Casitas
- History of the Peloponnesian War, the Napoleonic Wars, WWII
- Transcendentalism, Aristotelian philosophy
- Boldness, audacity, surprising people
- Wrestling, CrossFit, lifting weights, running
- Weight manipulation, nutrition, paleolithic diet
- Self-awareness, self-confidence, self-reliance
- Freedom, mobility, liquidity
- The 4-hour Workweek, Think and Grow Rich, The Power of Positive Thinking
- The end of the movie The Pursuit of Happyness when Chris Gardner gets the job and claps his hands to celebrate alone in the street
- Unrealistic goals, impatience, loopholes
- Entrepreneurship, product creation
- Fight Club, Five Easy Pieces, Rocky

- I can do all things through Christ who strengthens me
- The speech at the beginning of the movie *Patton*
- Unpredictability, random connections with people
- "Ideas are the beginning points of all fortunes"
  —Napoleon Hill
- Divine spark, indomitable spirit, conviction
- Unshakable, uncompromising, uncontainable
- Shaking things up, waking people from their daily stupor, stirring people's souls
- Christianity, God, Jesus, Paul, faith, belief
- Biochemistry, biology, anatomy, science
- Steve Jobs' Stanford Graduation speech
- Inner peace, enjoyment, being present
- The end of the movie *Shawshank Redemption* when Andy Dufresne escapes through the wall
- Passion, intensity, romance, adventure
- Mastery, autonomy, comraderie
- Starry Night by Vincent van Gogh
- Spontaneity, impulsiveness, pushing limits
- Einstein, physics, The History of the Universe
- Motivational speaking, Toastmasters, Joel Osteen
- Inspiring others, empowerment, triggering growth
- Slaughtering sacred cows, debunking conventional wisdom, creating tension, mixing it up
- Energy, enthusiasm, decisiveness
- Grit, tenacity, relentlessness, persistence
- "A man can be destroyed but not defeated."
  —Ernest Hemingway

Now, study and consolidate your list. What do the things on your list have in common? What words or short phrases could you use to describe them?

Identify at least a dozen words and short phrases that make you come alive on the inside. Do not settle for lukewarm words. Choose words that trigger an intensely positive emotional response. For example, instead of writing the word "Determined," write "Unstoppable." Instead of writing "Honesty," write "Absolute integrity." Here is the word list I came up with in 2010:

> Unrealistic expectations, Individuality,
> Energy, Unpredictability, Bold action,
> Purposeful connections, Striving impatiently,
> Indomitable spirit, Self-awareness, Fluidity,
> Romance, Vitality, Divine spark, Relentlessness,
> Strategy, Adventure, Curiosity

Now it's time to replace your old story with your new story. For this step, disengage your emotions and think about your life as level-headedly as possible. What is your current position? Where are you in life right now? In other words, what has been your life story up until now? Mentally pin down a description of your current place in the world as you see it. Consider your recent accomplishments and failures. Consider what you have, as well as what you lack. Write a few sentences encapsulating the current plot of your life.

Now, picture the life you want. Picture yourself achieving your goal and fulfilling your purpose. What does this new story look like? What actions are involved? How do you need to change your current story to match it? What words do you need to remove or change to turn your current story into your new story? On paper, transform your life as you see it now into the life you want to have in the future. Cross off words and insert new ones, delete storylines, and add sentences. Turn your current position into your future position. As you write your new story, act as if you are living it out right now. Write "I am ..." not "I will be ..." Here is how I changed my story in 2010 to a new story I could live immediately:

I am an ~~Anatomy and Cell Biology~~ (PhD) student *travels internationally* working to publish ~~an~~ academic article and trying to get a job as an applicaton scientist or (*biomedical consultant.*) I am going to Toastmasters to master public speaking and CrossFit to stay healthy, while volunteer coaching, creating my first inspirational product, and designing a website for my blog. *motivating others*

* running my own enterprises

I am a PhD and published author that travels internationally as a biomedical consultant. I am running my own enterprises, creating and releasing a new product annually. I am an inspirational speaker with a best-selling book, working daily to motivate others, become a better communicator and staying healthy.

Finally, emotionalize your new story. At this point you should have two things: a dozen words or short phrases that powerfully motivate you and the plot (or backbone) of your new life story. The final step is to hang your empowering words and phrases on the backbone of your new story. In other words, it's time to merge the soulful with the practical. Here is the final product of the new story I wrote for myself in 2010:

I am creating purposeful connections and maintaining my individuality and fluidity by consulting internationally. I am relentlessly and strategically running my own enterprises with bold action and an indomitable spirit, releasing a new product each year with unrealistic expectations for its success. I am a best-selling author and inspirational speaker known for igniting a divine spark in others, impatiently striving to increase vitality and self-awareness.

Notice the difference between my original story and its emotionally charged counterpart. My new story helped me reinterpret my life in a way that was consistent with my new purpose. Writing a new story for your life is the only way to give your life a new meaning. In the end, you should have a galvanizing personal story you strongly identify with. Your new story should be so inspiring that it fills you with confidence and an uncontrollable desire to act.

If you followed all of the above steps, be proud of yourself. It takes a great deal of initiative and courage to sit down and write out a new, inspiring mission for your life. If you didn't, it's not too late. Declare your new destiny as soon as possible.

Case Study

Lindsey Surace, MD

While in medical school, Lindsey Surace was on a mission. She was determined to save the world. Lindsey received her MD from Penn State University in Hershey, Pennsylvania and completed her residency and fellowship at Beth Israel Deaconess Medical Center in Boston, a Harvard teaching hospital. She scored in the top tenth percentile on Steps 2 and 3 of the Medical Licensing Examination as well as the American Board of Internal Medicine Licensing Examination. During her residency, Lindsey gave everything. She worked 80 hours a week, sacrificing her free time, friendships, and health to help her patients.

During the summer between her first and second years of medical school, Lindsey participated in the Uganda Village Project,[19] a humanitarian organization created by doctors to provide independent and impartial medical assistance to people in foreign countries whose survival is threatened by violence, neglect, or catastrophe. Lindsey planned to spend her summer in Uganda in East Africa, providing medical care firsthand to sick, starving, and dying families. Lindsey was so excited about the trip that she couldn't think of anything else. Finally, this was her chance to make a real difference and to be somebody.

While the experience was life-changing, the conditions in Uganda were abysmal. There was no running water. There was no trash collection, so rubbish was either burned or dumped in the streets, which were all dirt. There were hospitals in the town but patients had to bring their families to cook for them and pay for their own medication as it was being administered. No cash, no treatment. Many patients didn't even have enough money to travel to the hospital, let alone bring their family and pay for expensive treatments. For most patients, even bags of saline were too expensive. Lindsey felt like she was fighting an infinite battle. She wanted to save everyone but no matter how hard she worked, nothing improved. The crisis was much larger than what could be addressed by the direct care of patients. Lindsey was disheartened. She worked around the clock and didn't take time for herself. Suddenly, Lindsey realized she couldn't save the world. She couldn't even save Uganda. That's when Lindsey lost her drive.

Lindsey was telling herself a bad story: one that told her she could only be a successful doctor if she saved everyone in the worst possible conditions. It told her that the only way she could make a difference was to save the entire world, or at least an entire country. Lindsey needed a story that would allow her to take time for herself and was in line with her new purpose. After going to Uganda, Lindsey decided she no longer wanted to save the world. Instead, she wanted to help people in a way that was both meaningful and sustainable. This meant allowing herself to have a life outside of work. Lindsey realized that she could work hard and help less privileged families in America while making time for friends, family, and herself.

Lindsey changed her life by changing her story. First, she made a list of all of her sources of inspiration and then narrowed the list down into a few key words and phrases that sparked strong emotional reactions in her. Second, she created the backbone of her new story by writing down her old story, eliminating the unhealthy and disempowering parts, and adding new healthy and empowering sentences. Third, Lindsey added the emotionally charged words from the first step to her new story. The result was a story that sparked a sense of confidence, connection, purpose, and fulfillment in her.

Lindsey's old story was:

> The only way I can truly be a successful doctor is by saving the world and being recognized for it. Any time I take for myself is selfish.
> The only way for me to be a good person is to always help other people and always put their needs before mine. If I don't sacrifice everything to everyone else, I won't be remembered and my life will be a failure. If I leave the hospital to take a private practice position, I won't be able to stay at the cutting edge of my field and will be a failure.

Lindsey's new story was:

> I am already a magnificently successful doctor. I have already made a gigantic difference in the world. I have helped many people and deserve to take time for myself. The best way for me to take care of other people's health and wellbeing is to take care of my health and wellbeing first. I will be remembered for what I've already contributed. I am enthusiastically committed to being married, living in a beautiful home, and building a successful private practice. I am excited about staying on the cutting edge of my field while staying centered in my personal life.

Lindsey's old story made her feel selfish, unimportant, and unsuccessful. Conversely, her new story made her feel a sense of pride in her accomplishments, which gave her permission internally to take time for herself, her relationships, and her health. Lindsey's new story also clarified her new purpose, which was to get married, join a successful private practice in a male dominated field, start a family, and build a home close to her relatives in Pennsylvania.

In 2013, Lindsey acquired a private position in Gastroenterology at a well-established and successful practice, two years ahead of schedule. She recently purchased a large piece of property in Pennsylvania and enjoys spending her free time reading, jogging with her dog, and working on house plans with her husband.

Question Your Focus

....

"At the end of the day, the questions we ask of ourselves determine the type of people that we will become."

Leo Babauta

Questions focus the mind and inspire action. So far, you've worked in reverse order to find your purpose by making a wish list of actions, naming your new position, defining your priorities, and rewriting your story. As a result, you've aimed yourself directly at your desired finish line. You've found your mountain peak and are ready to start moving towards it. The next steps involve mapping out your path to the peak. Achieving any worthwhile goal requires constant aiming. The only way to fulfill your purpose in life is to stay pointed towards it. This means you have to stay focused and motivated. Without one or the other, your progress will quickly slow, or—worse—stop altogether.

Questions point you towards your purpose

Chester Santos calls himself the international man of memory.[20] He was crowned the 2008 USA National Memory Champion[21] and currently provides corporate training in the fields of memory improvement and mental fitness. In business, remembering people's names is a critical part of networking and relationship-building. But it can be difficult. Matching a large number of names to prominent faces in a large field gives a lot of professionals trouble. Santos says the fix is easy; he tells clients to start asking questions. In 2013, I interviewed Santos and asked him to describe his method. This is what he had to say:

> *"As soon as you meet someone new, use their name in a sentence. Then, ask them a question using their name ... And start asking yourself questions too. Ask, 'What is unique about this*

person?' ... Also ask, 'What is familiar about this person? What about this person reminds me of someone I already know?' Asking questions and linking their name to many different parts of your brain will help you remember it forever."

Santos' method for remembering names works, in part, because asking questions is a powerful way to focus your mind. In the same way, you can use Santos' method to direct your mental energies towards your purpose in life.

Change the questions that you are asking yourself and you will change your focus. Chapter 2 of this book explained how the question, "How can I escape?" inspired and motivated Stanislavsky Lech to break out of a Nazi death camp in Krakow, risking his life in the process. Chapter 7 showed how Alexander Selkirk was able to survive after being shipwrecked on a deserted island by changing the questions he asked from, "Why me?" and "What do I need?" to "What do I have, right here and right now?" Chapter 11 explained how asking questions that were in line with my new core priorities helped me change the direction of my life. I stopped asking myself, "How can I get ahead?" and started asking myself, "How can I add value?" and "How can I contribute more?"

> **Change the questions that you are asking yourself and you will change your focus.**

Questions become obsessions

Every goal I ever achieved, or came close to achieving, was simply the answer to a question I was obsessively asking myself. In high school, I asked myself, "How can I be a wrestling State champion?" over and over again until I made it to the State tournament. Every semester I asked myself, "How can I be a valedictorian?" until I was standing behind the podium at my high school graduation, giving the valedictorian speech.

In graduate school, I asked myself, "How can I get out of here with my PhD as soon as possible?" until I graduated. These questions kept me focused on my goals and motivated me to take action to achieve them. If you ask yourself a difficult question enough times, you will find a way to answer it.

Questions are tools

Questions have the power to shift your focus instantly and fill you with energy and inspiration. The first thing you need to do is identify the questions you are currently asking yourself. Which questions consume you on a daily basis? Are they productive? If not, change your questions. You control the questions you ask.

Use questions to stay focused on your new direction in life. Throughout the day, ask yourself, "What is my purpose?" "What are my core priorities?" and "What is my story?" Avoid distractions by asking, "What is the most important thing I can do right now?" and "Will this matter in a year from now?" Stay positive by asking, "What's great about this situation right now?" Use quality questions to get quality answers and quality results.

17

Create a Personal Slogan

"That the powerful play goes on, and you may contribute a verse."

Walt Whitman

Your life is a statement. I was at 10,000 feet, hiking up to the summit of Vail Mountain. It was a cool fall day but I was sweating like a pig and gasping for air. Earlier that morning, I decided to rent a mountain bike and ride it up the mountain and back down. This quickly turned into a decision to walk the bike up the mountain and try to stay alive long enough to ride it back down. When I finally hit the summit, my blood was pumping hard and my thoughts were moving a mile a minute. I was thinking about how amazing it felt to be outside and how much I loved pushing myself physically. I was also thinking I better not die climbing this mountain because I have a lot more life left to live.

Then, a question popped into my head: "If you died right now, what would you stand for?" The question caught me off guard so I stopped and thought for a minute. I was really asking myself, "What is your life philosophy?" Inspired, I unzipped the trunk bag on the bike, pulled out my iPhone, and typed the following note:

You cannot fulfill your purpose in life without connecting your personal identity to it.

> *"My philosophy is to seek out the best things in life and then learn, seize, experience, and enjoy those things with enthusiasm, confidence, and vitality. Once you've had your fill, take a break and teach others how to do the same, and when you get sick of teaching, set out on a new adventure and start the process all over again."*

Your personal philosophy is the unabridged version of your personal slogan. It is the song you live your life by. Over the next several weeks, I kept thinking about the words I wrote that day in Vail. I wish I had written them down a long time ago. Having a philosophy on life, a credo, dramatically clarified my purpose of living. But I wasn't satisfied. I wanted more clarity. I wanted to reduce my song down to a single lyric. Here's what I came up with: "My mission is to contribute massively, build strong relationships, and live like a lion."

Be a player, not a pawn

No one can opt out of having a mission. Whether or not you're aware of it, you've chosen a mission for your life and you are carrying it out right now. Even those who choose to eat, sleep, and live in front of a TV are on a mission. Their mission is sloth. Their mission statement is to be slothful. Either passively or actively, as a pawn or player, you are living out a mission; the key is to choose it dynamically. By doing so, you will command your life rather than be commanded by it.

A personal slogan will help fully develop the bond between your purpose and your identity.

Life can destroy you, but not defeat you. There may be times when your mission is influenced by uncontrollable circumstances, but you can always control your attention and your attitude. You can have your health, wealth, and relationships taken from you, but not your awareness, ambition, and hope. This is why creating a crystal clear vision for your future is so important. By carefully mapping your priorities, story, and questions, you can stay focused on your purpose of living even when your circumstances change.

You cannot fulfill your purpose in life without connecting your personal identity to it. This is why writing a new life story is important to achieving your goal. But stories are not enough; you need a life philosophy. You need a mission statement, or slogan, to live your life by. A personal slogan will help fully develop the bond between your purpose and your identity.

Make a statement

Your slogan is a personal mission statement for your life. It will help you make major, life-changing decisions, and it will help you make daily decisions in the midst of distractions. Steven Covey, author of *The 7 Habits of Highly Effective People*,[22] gives the following advice for writing a mission statement:

1 Write down your roles as you now see them. Are you satisfied with the mirror image of your life?

2 Start a collection of notes, quotes, and ideas you may want to use as resource material in writing your personal mission statement.

3 Identify a project you will be facing in the near future and apply the principle of mental creation. Write down the results you desire.

In previous chapters, I've shown you how to do all three of the above steps. If you've taken the time to write your purpose, priorities, story, and question, then you have everything you need to write a powerful slogan for your life. Carefully review these items until you pick up on the central theme for who you want to be and what you want your life to look like. Trim the fat from your new purpose and your new identity until you arrive at their essence. This should be something you can describe in a sentence.

A slogan is a lyric, not a lecture

Do not make the mistake of turning your mission statement into a paragraph of uninspiring jargon that no one—not even yourself—can or will remember. Here are some examples of what NOT to do:

"We are committed to being the world's premier petroleum and petrochemical company. To that end, we must continuously achieve superior financial and operating results while adhering to the highest standards of business conduct. These

unwavering expectations provide the foundation for our commitments to those with whom we interact."

- ExxonMobil[23]

"Harvard strives to create knowledge, to open the minds of students to that knowledge, and to enable students to take best advantage of their educational opportunities. To these ends, the College encourages students to respect ideas and their free expression, and to rejoice in discovery and in critical thought; to pursue excellence in a spirit of productive cooperation; and to assume responsibility for the consequences of personal actions. Harvard seeks to identify and to remove restraints on students' full participation, so that individuals may explore their capabilities and interests and may develop their full intellectual and human potential. Education at Harvard should liberate students to explore, to create, to challenge, and to lead. The support the College provides to students is a foundation upon which self-reliance and habits of lifelong learning are built: Harvard expects that the scholarship and collegiality it fosters in its students will lead them in their later lives to advance knowledge, to promote understanding, and to serve society."

Harvard College[24]

Your mission statement is not a rant, a lecture, or a lesson plan. It's not a way of getting respect, attention, or admiration. Your slogan is a catchy song lyric that stays stuck in your head. It's a beating drum that keeps your life in cadence with your life's task. It's a giant thumping mallet crashing down on your head when you get distracted. Don't write a slogan for other people or one that's safe and reasonable. Most importantly, don't write some long statement you can't remember. Write something that makes you leap on the inside. In the end, your slogan should be brief and bold, totally exposing who you are and what you want.

When writing your statement, use powerful action verbs that arouse your emotions. Also, use descriptive words that convey many meanings at once. I ended my mission statement with "live like a lion." To me, these four words represent a way of living that includes being present and cheerful, eating a primal diet and working out intensely, and taking time to rest and sleep well. Keep trimming your slogan down to its central core. Once you have a lyric that feels like it's a part of you, play it in your head over and over again. In this way, your slogan will keep you focused on your mission.

18

Start a Meme

"Words can be like X-rays if you use them properly—
they'll go through anything."

Aldous Huxley

The meme is the new mission statement. I've found that a personal slogan is great for keeping me focused when it's written down in front of me. I keep my slogan on my computer desktop and on my bathroom mirror. However, due to its length, this slogan loses its impact when I'm in the midst of activities involving other people and quickly changing circumstances. Even though "contribute massively, build strong relationships, and live like a lion" is only one, short sentence, it can be difficult and awkward to repeat to myself internally when I'm engaged in the real world.

In the midst of battle, you need something versatile to keep your focus. You need a word or phrase that is simple and mobile. You need a word that cuts deep into your psyche and will immediately impact your decisions and actions. You need a meme. A meme is a "word, phrase, idea, or behavior that spreads from person to person within a culture. [It] acts as a unit for carrying cultural ideas, symbols or practices, which can be transmitted from one mind to another through writing, speech, gestures, rituals or other imitable phenomena."[25]

In the midst of battle, you need something versatile to keep your focus.

One word can change an entire organization. In *The Power of Habit*,[26] author Charles Duhigg discusses how an untested CEO named Paul O'Neil took over Alcoa Inc., one of the largest manufacturing companies in America. His first order of business was redefining the company's mission. Safety became the firm's top priority. Every operating procedure was built around increasing safety. The entire company, from the top down, was reorganized to improve safety.

Lines of communication were improved, dress codes were altered, and factory equipment was upgraded—all to maximize safety. Soon, safety turned into a meme that percolated throughout the entire organization. *Safety* was their mission. *Safety* brought everyone together. Eventually, *safety* came to define the organization. As a result of these changes, Alcoa became the top performer in the Dow Jones.

A meme is a virus

A strong meme will transmit your slogan throughout every part of your life. When I started my post-graduate school career as an Application Scientist, I started using the word "bring" to motivate and focus my colleagues, as well as myself. I used it as a kind of one-word war drum to engage everyone. Over time, this meme shifted the attitude of the entire company. It became the answer to everyone's problems. What do we do when morale is low? Bring. What do we do if an order is messed up? Bring. Hiring managers started hiring people who brought it hard. People started to communicate more. Everyone's creative energy flowed.

A strong meme will transmit your slogan throughout every part of your life.

After a few months, everyone had a different *bring* name. There was Steve Bringfontaine, Bring Kong, Marilyn Bringroe, and Arnold Schwarzebringer. In my own life, I continue to use this word to keep me focused.

Bring encapsulates my mission to contribute as much as possible, to develop strong and lasting relationships, and always to live like a lion. I use this word to inject my slogan into every part of my life and to keep me focused when things get tough. Find a meme you identify with and that infects everything that you do.

19

Put a Compelling Vision in Front of You

··

"The greatest danger for most of us is not that our aim is too high and we miss it, but that it is too low and we reach it."

Michelangelo di Lodovico Buonarroti Simoni

Tara Holland had always dreamed of becoming Miss America. In 1994, she entered the Miss Florida pageant and won first runner-up. The next year, Tara entered the same contest and, once again, was announced first runner-up. Instead of giving up, Tara stayed focused on achieving her goal. In 1997, after moving to Kansas, she entered the Miss Kansas pageant and won the title. That same year, she went on to be crowned Miss America. After the Miss America pageant, a reporter asked Tara if she was nervous walking down the runway in front of millions of people watching on television and with the announcer singing the famous Miss America song.

"No, I wasn't nervous at all," she said. "I had walked down that runway thousands of times before."

In another interview, Tara told how after losing twice in a row at the state level, she had rented dozens of videos of local pageants, state pageants, Miss Teen, Miss Universe, Miss World, and whatever else she could get her hands on, and watched them repeatedly. As she watched each woman get crowned the winner, she pictured herself in that situation. She imagined herself receiving the crown and walking down the runway. When her vision became a reality, she had already made that walk a thousand times. This story is told in *Your Best Life Now*,[27] written by Joel Osteen. The message of the story is simple: creating a compelling and tangible vision for your future will pull you towards achieving your goals. The more compelling the vision, the stronger you will be pulled towards your purpose.

The more compelling the vision, the stronger you will be pulled towards your purpose.

Get a bigger frying pan. I heard a story about a man fishing by a river. A small boy walked up and watched the man as he threw his lure. Soon after, a fish tugged at the man's fishing pole. After reeling in his line, the man pulled a 24-inch fish out of the water and abruptly threw it back in. A few minutes later, the man caught another massive fish and immediately threw it back in. This continued until the kid finally asked, "Why are you throwing all of those big fish back?" The man replied, "Because I only have a ten-inch frying pan." You have to make room in your thinking for your biggest goals before your life will make room for them.

Create a compelling vision

Your vision should be big and bold: something that inspires action and influences motivation. It should be the visual depiction—the visual manifestation—of every step we've talked about up to this point. It should include things that you want to have, be, and do. If you haven't done so already, brainstorm at least a dozen things you dream of having (house, car, clothing, cash), being (a great marathon runner, fluent in French), and doing (sky dive, travel the world, run with the bulls in Pamplona) in the next five to ten years. Then, do the same exercise for things that you want to have, be, and do in the next six to 12 months.

Bringing your dreams to life on paper will help you bring them to life in reality. This includes taking the time to write down your new purpose, priorities, story, questions, and slogan. If you've done these things, then you've already created a compelling vision for your future. Now all you have to do is make it tangible by creating a vision board.

You have to make room in your thinking for your biggest goals before your life will make room for them.

In the book *Stop Talking, Start Doing*,[28] Shaa Wasmund recounts the story of Conrad Hilton, who, during the Great Depression, clipped out a picture of the newly completed Waldorf-Astoria Hotel in New York. Later, when he had enough cash to buy a desk, he put the picture under the desk's glass top so that he could look at it every day. In 1949, almost two decades later, Hilton bought the famous hotel.

How to create a vision board

Expose your soul. Add depth to your desires. The key to creating a compelling and tangible vision board is posting pictures of both your short-term and long-term goals. As you start achieving your goals, a healthy tension will be created between what you have accomplished and what you have yet to accomplish. On the one side, you will have specific achievements that you can identify with presently. On the other side, you will have goals that you are in the process of achieving. The merging of these two sides into one concrete vision will generate tension and energy, which will continuously pull you forward towards your dreams.

First, name your purpose. Either type the name of one of your biggest life goals or cut out a pictorial representation of it. Then, post it directly in the center of your board. In 2010, my purpose in life was getting out of graduate school and starting my career in business and entrepreneurship. My dream was to one day run my own enterprises, creating products and impactful services. I captured this dream simply by typing out "Isaiah Hankel Enterprises" and posting it on my board. My second biggest goal was to have perfectly healthy kidneys. I had recently been diagnosed with a kind of kidney disease called IgA nephropathy and stopping, or reversing, its progression was a new priority (you can read more in the Preface). I created a vision for this by cutting out a picture of a healthy glomeruli (a network of capillaries in the kidney that is critical for filtering blood) and pasting it to the center of my board.

After posting your largest, long-term goals in the center of your board, start posting your short-term goals. Fill in the periphery of your board, first with your five- to ten-year goals, and then with your six- to 12-month goals. In total, I suggest posting one to three major life goals in the center, followed by several five- to ten year goals and several six- to 12-month goals.

On my 2010 vision board, I posted pictures of houses, cars, boats, jets, and blocks of cold hard cash, all of which I wanted to have in five to ten years. In graduate school, I was living a lifestyle full of lack and debt. These pictures were meant to help me remove any and all mental limits from my life. For the same five- to ten-year timeline, I posted the phrase "The Isaiah Hankel Wrestling Foundation," which symbolized my dream to start a scholarship fund for high school wrestlers. I also posted pictures of experiences that I wanted to have in the next five to ten years, including owning a villa in Croatia. For my six- to 12-month goals, I posted pictures of things that I wanted to do immediately after graduating, including scuba diving, rock climbing, and traveling the world. Finally, I pasted pictures of people who inspired me to work hard, as well as quotes and empowering words that focused me and motivated me to take action.

Show off your vision

After I finished creating my vision board, I hung it up on the wall above my desk. I was living in a friend's basement at the time, which meant that my living room, office, and bedroom were all the same room. As a result, anyone who visited me was able to see my vision board. At first, I was embarrassed by it and would hang up a sheet or towel over it when my friends visited. But, as time went on, I got used to it. I became less and less concerned with what other people thought and showed it off openly.

Creating a vision board not only helped me stay focused and motivated; it also helped me become more open, honest, and authentic. My vision board wasn't a symbol of some image I wanted to show off; it was my heart and soul. Last year, I created a new vision board that included a list of my new priorities, story, questions, and personal slogan. If you've taken the time to write these things out for yourself, be sure to include them in your vision board.

20

Turn Your Vision into a Decision

"Crying is all right in its own way while it lasts. But you have to stop sooner or later, and then you still have to decide what to do."

C.S. Lewis

A simple decision can give you life, or it can give you death. Numerous anthropologists who have lived with primitive people in South America, Africa, Australia, New Zealand, and Haiti have reported several incidences of "voodoo" death where, for example, a tribal witch doctor kills a healthy member of the tribe merely by pointing a "death bone" at him.[29] Scientists have spent years trying to understand such instances of psychogenic or psychosomatic death, where people kill themselves with the power of their own mind.[30]

Every high school wrestling season, my coach told the team a story of a man who worked for a meatpacking company loading and unloading massive freight lockers. After the lockers were filled with meat, they would be sealed shut and transported nationally by train. One day, after the man finished loading a series of lockers, he accidentally sealed himself in the last one. He banged and banged on the door but no one could hear him. Suddenly the train started to move. The man had worked on the line for more than 20 years so he knew exactly how much oxygen was in the locker and how much time he had before he would die. He even knew the symptoms he would experience as he ran out of oxygen. With a little flashlight attached to his keychain, the man kept a journal of his thoughts for his family.

The next day, the man's dead body and journal were discovered in the train. The first few pages of the journal read well, with loving notes to his wife and children. Then, in the middle of the journal, the man's sentences started to break apart and not make sense. Finally, the last few pages of the journal were filled with chicken scratch that was completely unintelligible. After inspecting the locker, the freight crew found a long crack along the base of the back wall where it came together with the floor. The locker wasn't sealed. There would have been plenty of oxygen in the locker for 20 men. Later, the police and crew tested the locker's broken seal with an oxygen monitor and found that the oxygen levels were not affected by closing the door. Yet the autopsy showed that the man died of oxygen deprivation, matching his progressively decreased ability to write coherently in his journal.

Mind over matter

If your mind is powerful enough to kill you, it's also powerful enough to give you the life you want. Eutimo Perez used to live in extreme pain, suffering from the degenerative joint disease osteoarthritis, which is characterized by the breakdown of the cartilage in joints. But then Perez took part in a clinical trial designed to test the efficacy of arthroscopic surgery on osteoarthritic knees and has been pain-free for more than two years since.[31,32] Here's the interesting thing: Perez never received the surgery. He was in the "sham surgery," or placebo group, of a study testing whether arthroscopic knee surgery actually relieved patient pain or if it was "all in their heads." During the study, the members of the first group received the actual arthroscopic procedure, where damaged cartilage is scraped or flushed out with the aid of a thin viewing scope. Members of the second group were merely given anesthesia and two incisions on their knees to *look* as though an arthroscope had been inserted. After the surgeries, both groups reported improvement in knee function and a complete loss of pain. The second group simply saw the fake incisions and decided to feel better.

Decide what you want and your mind will find a way to get it

It's not enough to decide on a goal; you have to decide to reach it.

You have to decide to take what you want. No one is coming to give it to you.

When I was in high school, my biggest goal in life was to be a State champion wrestler. I trained relentlessly all year round, sacrificing every night and weekend to the sport of wrestling while my classmates partied and hung out at the mall. I worked swing shifts at the local grocery store after evening practice to pay for summer wrestling camps and off-season tournaments. I did everything I was supposed to do. Yet, I fell short. I lost by a point in the quarterfinals of the State tournament in my senior year, killing my dream once and for all. Looking back, I realize that part of me thought I would achieve my goal just by doing all the right things. I subconsciously expected life to hand me a gold medal in payment for my loyalty to the system.

> **Your vision will remain a fantasy until you decide to transform it into reality. Without a decision, your vision is a pipe dream. It's wishful thinking.**

You have to open the door to success yourself. Doing all the right things and working hard will get you to the doorstep, but you still have to reach out, grab the handle, and push the door open. This requires a firm decision to see your mission all the way through to the end. It also requires you to believe in yourself with the utmost intensity. On your way to achieving your goal, you have to completely engross yourself in extreme feelings of confidence and accomplishment. You have to absolutely know you are going to fulfill your purpose in life. And you have to be your own source of fulfillment. No one is coming to save or validate you. This is because no one else can live your life for you. Plus, everyone else is in the process of pursuing their own dreams, and rightly so. Sure, people can support you along the way, but they can't make you feel a sense of growth and accomplishment. Other people can give you rewards and access to experiences, but they can't *experience* things for you. Feelings of achievement and fulfillment must come from within.

A vision can be turned into a conviction by making a firm decision to achieve it, amplifying your belief in that decision, and validating that decision repeatedly. I effectively applied this principle in graduate school to receive my PhD. Refusing to repeat the mistake I made in high school, I left nothing to chance and attacked my goal from every angle until the degree itself was in my hands. I didn't wait for it to be given to me; I took it. During my last two years of graduate school, I was consistently told "Not yet" by my mentor, or given a blank stare by my thesis committee whenever I asked for permission to graduate. Nevertheless, I started writing my thesis and applying for PhD-level jobs. I changed my email signature to "Isaiah Hankel, PhD" and changed my outgoing phone message to "You've reached the voicemail of Dr Isaiah Hankel …" I told companies I interviewed with to call my mentor and tell him they were excited for me to get my degree. I talked with every dean and professor on campus about my pending graduation. I made a decision and arranged the world around me to match it. I cut myself off from any other option. Then, one day, out of the blue, my mentor told me to turn in my thesis and set a date to defend it and graduate.

A decision is the link between wanting something to happen and making something happen. Your vision will remain a fantasy until you decide to transform it into reality. Without a decision, your vision is a pipe dream. It's wishful thinking. This is how most people live their entire lives, hoping for something to happen but never deciding to make it happen. Their goals are better described as wishes. Their visions are hallucinations. You can be different by making the decision to fulfill your purpose, align yourself with your priorities, live your story, answer your questions, and personify your slogan. Cut yourself off from any other option. By making this decision, you will automatically raise your mind's expectations. You will bring the full breadth of your mental powers to attention.

21

Move from Decision to Conviction

"Expectancy is the atmosphere for miracles."

Edwin Louis Cole

The Pygmalion effect is a phenomenon where the greater the expectation placed upon a person, the better he or she performs.[33] In 1968, Robert Rosenthal and Lenore Jacobson performed an experiment where they gave every student in a single California elementary school a disguised IQ test without disclosing the scores to the school's teachers.[34] The teachers were told that some of their students (about 20% of the school chosen at random) could be expected to be "spurters" that year, doing better than expected in comparison to their classmates. In reality, these spurters had the same or lower IQs than the other students. The spurters' names were made known to the teachers. At the end of the study, every student was again tested with the same IQ test. The result? The spurters showed large gains compared to everyone else, even though their initial IQ scores were the same or lower. Rosenthal and Jacobson concluded that merely increasing expectations can dramatically enhance achievement.

Expectations are your ticket to a self-fulfilling prophecy

In order to fulfill your new purpose in life, you must dramatically increase your expectations. Once you decide on a goal, you need to decide to achieve it. This means you must increase your expectations. You have to expect to achieve your goal. Expecting achievement is very different than hoping and dreaming for something to come true. Expectation requires a much higher level of commitment and emotion. A decision is only as strong as the belief standing behind it. You have to expect you are going to achieve your goal and fulfill your purpose in life. And this belief has to be backed with irresistible intensity: you will not fail; there is no other option; this is the mountain you will die on. The fastest and most effective way to create this kind of intensity is through a process called superimposition.

The process of superimposition

Narrow your mind. Superimpose the passion you feel for a conviction that is already present in your life onto your new belief. A decision to achieve a new goal creates a new belief—the belief that you can achieve it. Next, you need to turn your new belief into a powerful conviction that shouts: you will achieve it! A real conviction will make you feel as though you already have your goal in hand, right now—as if tightening your grip is all that's left to do.

Believe you are going to achieve your goal with the same intensity that you believe in your political and religious viewpoints. Most people's strongest convictions fall into the realm of religion and politics. People with these kinds of convictions spend their lives finding new ways to back up their beliefs. Consider someone you know who believes without a shadow of a doubt that something is true. This person probably spends his or her entire life finding things to back up this belief while refusing to entertain alternative viewpoints for very long, if at all. *Voilà*: that's exactly what you need to do to turn your decision into a conviction.

A decision is only as strong as the belief standing behind it.

Think of your strongest conviction, the one belief that you know in your heart is true. Really let yourself feel it. Once you have a feeling for it, apply that feeling towards your new goal. Superimpose those exact emotions onto your new purpose in life. This process will help unify your priorities, story, question, and slogan. Superimposition will multiply the pull of your new purpose in life.

22

Celebrate Your Progress

"The more you celebrate your life, the more there is in life to celebrate."

Oprah Winfrey

Celebrate every win. Strengthen and maintain your conviction by building references and consistently validating yourself. Once you've turned your vision into a conviction, seek all of the information that you can find on why you are capable of achieving your goal. Ask yourself, "What have I done in the past that's already prepared me for fulfilling my new purpose?" and "What can I learn or do, right now, to bring me closer to achieving my goal?" Learn the art of celebrating yourself. As you continue to build references and generate momentum towards your goal, take time to savor every win. Inspiration is perishable; celebration is the best way to keep it alive.

Motivate yourself daily

You need to find ways to motivate yourself daily; otherwise your conviction will start to atrophy. Stop waiting for the world around you to take notice and validate your own victories. At the end of every day, review your accomplishments and take a moment to acknowledge that you are one day closer to achieving your goal. Keep setting and annihilating new benchmarks so that you always have something to celebrate.

Most of the time, even when you accomplish something worthwhile, no one will notice. Your biggest victories in life probably won't look like the last scene in *Rudy*, where Rudy Ruettiger is carried off the Notre Dame football field while thousands of people chant his name.[35] Instead, it will look like the last scene in *The Pursuit*

Inspiration is perishable; celebration is the best way to keep it alive.

of Happyness, when Chris Gardner is offered the paid position at the brokerage firm, concluding his one-year internship and getting him and his son off of the streets. Gardner shakes hands with the managers, walks out of the building completely alone, and triumphantly claps his hands to himself.[36] The obstacle is the path. On the way to achieving your goal, no one will ever know just how hard you've worked. No one can possibly peer into your mind, body, and soul to understand how much of yourself you've sacrificed to your vision. So stop expecting them to. Personal growth is your victory. Celebrate it.

23

Run the Numbers Behind Your Vision

"What gets measured gets managed."

Peter Drucker

Alarge amount of cash may not be required for you to fulfill your purpose in life, but it can definitely make things easier. Money creates options and removes obstacles. No matter what your purpose in life is, I would bet that increasing cash flow would help fulfill it faster. The key is first to name your purpose, define your priorities, write your story, and completely map out your new direction in life.

Establish your destiny without considering money

Create your vision without any limits whatsoever. Then, run the numbers. Once you've turned your vision into a conviction, calculate what your conviction will cost. For this, I recommend moving from annual thinking (I make $50,000 a year and need to make $100,000 a year) to daily thinking (I make $137 a day and need to make $274 a day). This is the income you will need to achieve your goals and to fulfill your ultimate purpose. In *The 4-Hour Work Week*, Tim Ferriss writes that your ideal lifestyle can only be achieved by moving from annual thinking to daily cash flow thinking.[37] Analyzing your needs and objectives by the day versus by the year will give you a visceral feel for what your days are currently worth and what you need to do to increase their worth. This kind of immediate analysis will put you in the present moment and will inspire you to think creatively.

Map your desired daily income with short-term benchmarks

This process will attach a purpose and a timeline to your cash flow goal. For example, what daily income do I need to hire a personal assistant, hike through Australia and New Zealand for two months, launch a successful blog, buy a Ducati and a new house, and live like a millionaire in Paris for a week? Is it $3,000 a day? Or perhaps $2,000 a day?, or $1,000? Nope. I only need to make $141 a day.

Money creates options and removes obstacles.

If I want to pay off everything in 12 months, including the house, I only need to make $410 a day.

These numbers seem surprisingly small because we are so used to thinking in terms of years. Stop being retirement-minded. You can live the life of your dreams right now. Could you find a way to make $140 today? Ask yourself the following questions: "What useless item can I sell?"; "What temporary job can I find?"; "What side project can I start?"; "What service or product can I turn into an online business?" If you have a job, you may only need $50 a day extra—or less—to live your retirement fantasies. Act as if your life depends on making that extra $50. Find a way. Leave no stone unturned. Let the immediacy of your daily objective fill you with a sense of urgency.

Case Study: Brenda Jones, JD

Brenda Jones wanted to live a full life, but she didn't know how. In high school and college she found herself taking tough classes and choosing a tough major because she was a typical type-A, first-born child, and it was expected. As the child of two health-care professionals, Brenda wanted to follow in her parents' footsteps by pursuing a pre-medical degree in college. But she wasn't thrilled with the classes. So, after a summer internship, Brenda chose to pursue a double major in Business and Literature. She felt a double major was a good first step to meeting everyone else's expectations. After a particularly stressful college summer, one of Brenda's professors encouraged her to take the Law School Admission Test (LSAT). If she didn't want to be a doctor, maybe she could be a lawyer instead. So, as graduation loomed, Brenda started to pursue a legal career.

Brenda was very successful in law school, which wasn't easy. As with most legal programs, the first year was dedicated to weeding out those who couldn't cut it. On the first day of class, the professors told the students to look to their left and their right, informing them that one of these two other students wouldn't make it to graduation. To make matters worse, the school had a policy: all scholarships for those who ranked in the bottom 50% of the class would be eliminated. Brenda wasn't sure she wanted to be a lawyer, but she worked hard to stay in the top third of her class. She chased and captured every carrot held in front of her. But she didn't really know where she was going. She had a nagging sense that a traditional, associate position at a local law firm would not fulfill her.

One day, Brenda decided to talk with her mentor about alternate career paths. But when Brenda suggested taking a job in corporate law or experimenting with a transactional position, her mentor said, "You probably won't graduate anyway."

Brenda responded to this challenge by forgetting the nagging feeling in her gut and working harder than ever. She would get an associate position. She would show her mentor who was right.

Brenda graduated from law school and started working in a small law firm. For Brenda, the best part of working at the firm was "learning what she did NOT want to do with her life." Doing research and paperwork for up to 12 hours a day was not fulfilling. Sitting in a small office and drafting briefs was not Brenda's purpose in life. Brenda was stuck. But how did she get here? She had done everything she was supposed to do. She worked hard, met every challenge, and even proved her mentor wrong. So why was she miserable?

Eventually, Brenda took some time to evaluate her purpose and her priorities. She recognized that she wanted an opportunity to travel and see the world. She also wanted to have time for a husband and a family. It was time to make a change.

Brenda started asking herself some new questions. She stopped asking, "What am I expected to do?" and instead started asking, "What's the best thing I can do?" and "How will this help me live a full life?"

Next, Brenda started creating a concrete vision for her future. She created a personal slogan: *To travel, build a family, be true to myself, and have fun*. Then she shortened her slogan into a meme: *family and fun first*. Finally, to keep her intensely focused on the future she wanted, Brenda created a vision board.

Brenda's vision board turned into a trophy case. Every time she lived out one of the items on her vision board, like traveling to a new country, she celebrated it by having a glass of wine, getting a pedicure, or purchasing a new cookbook. Every celebration added intensity to her decision to change and to her conviction to live a full life.

Two months after making her vision board, Brenda was hired into a government position that allowed her to travel the world extensively (and on the company dime) and be closer to family and friends. In the past four years she has advanced to a management position and is responsible for overseeing a large portfolio of government contracts. Recently, Brenda had her first son. She currently lives a full life with her husband and family, doing something she loves and staying true to her vision and personal slogan.

Brenda Jones is an alias used to protect the identity of the person behind this case study because they do secured access work.

PART THREE

How to Fulfill Your Purpose

"In the name of the best within you, do not sacrifice this world to those who are its worst. In the name of the values that keep you alive, do not let your vision of man be distorted by the ugly, the cowardly, the mindless in those who have never achieved his title. Do not lose your knowledge that man's proper estate is an upright posture, an intransigent mind and a step that travels unlimited roads. Do not let your fire go out, spark by irreplaceable spark, in the hopeless swamps of the approximate, the not-quite, the not-yet, the not-at-all. Do not let the hero in your soul perish in lonely frustration for the life you deserved, but have never been able to reach. Check your road and the nature of your battle. The world you desired can be won, it exists, it is real, it is possible, it's yours."

Ayn Rand

24

Pursue Mastery

"If you're any good at all, you know you can be better."

Lindsay Buckingham

Parts One and Two of this book were written with the assumption that you have a desire to be great; that you want to achieve mastery over some area of your life. If you have no such desire, then naming your purpose and mapping a new direction for your life are unnecessary. But if you want to achieve mastery, whether it is in the realm of business and entrepreneurship or of personal development, you have to stick to your new direction. Mastery is your mountain peak. Anything worth achieving requires focus and effort over a long period of time. You have to spend many hours, days, and even years generating momentum towards a single goal. This is why it is so important to pick a mountain peak that offers you an enjoyable journey. Contrary to popular belief, there are no real shortcuts to greatness.

Greatness is achieved by applying correct principles

Every year, countless books fill the shelves at bookstores promising to help you achieve mastery overnight. Since finishing graduate school, I've gone through an average of eight business and personal development bestsellers every month. This means I've read more than 300 non-fiction books over the past two years.

All of this reading has taught me two things. First, there are hundreds of ways to repackage the same *principle*; and second, by the time a new *process* is published, it's no longer cutting edge. When reading a recent non-fiction bestseller, focus on the principles, not the processes. In today's world, the only way to stay on the cutting

Mastery is your mountain peak. edge of new processes in your field is to network online through blogs and social media channels, as well as in person at conferences and other live events.

Action is the source of mastery

Reading non-fiction is critical for learning, building references, seeing new opportunities, and expanding your overall perspective. However, reading by itself will not help you achieve mastery. You have to apply the principles you learn and take action: specifically, purposeful action, in a single direction, for a long period of time. This means you will have to fail firsthand rather than succeed only in your imagination. Failing firsthand once will teach you more than reading a thousand books about other people succeeding. The risk of looking stupid or incompetent in a real-life situation has a way of snapping your brain to attention. There are immediate consequences. Your brain gets immediate feedback.

During my sophomore year of college, two of my wrestling teammates used to skip the long-distance runs that our coach made us do early in the season. In fact, they wouldn't try very hard during our team's technique or lifting sessions either. But when it came time to wrestle live matches at the end of practice, they brought it hard. They were consistently the toughest people in the room to win live matches against. Whether they wrestled live matches at the beginning or end of practice, or in an actual dual or tournament, they were fully engaged. Anything else, though, was considered a waste of their time. Our coaches resented them for this. To be honest, I did too.

But looking back, I realized that their behavior carried with it an important principle. The best way to get better at doing something is to do it, not to do things related to it. This lesson held true for me two years later when I was studying for the Medical College Admission Test (MCAT). Instead of studying the traditional way by reading expensive books and taking classes, I just took as many practice tests as possible. That year I scored higher than the previous year when I spent more than \$2,000 on a Kaplan Test Prep course[1] that included reading a dozen different books and sitting through extra classes every weekend. Failing firsthand is the best way to get the feedback you need to achieve mastery.

The best way to get better at doing something is to do it, not to do things related to it.

25

Acknowledge the 10,000-Hour Rule, but Don't Follow It

"Timing, perseverance and ten years of trying will eventually make you look like an overnight success."

Biz Stone

The 10,000-hour rule is the idea that it takes approximately 10,000 hours of deliberate practice to master a skill. For example, it would take ten years of practicing three hours a day to master a particular subject. Similarly, it would take about five years of full-time employment to become an expert in a given field. Studies of human performance in fields as different as chess, music, sports, surgery, and mathematics have shown that this rule holds true.

Outliers by Malcolm Gladwell[2] and *Talent Is Overrated* by Geoff Colvin[3] discuss this rule in detail. In the latter book, Colvin discusses experiments with virtuoso violinists, chess masters, and pro golfers, showing a direct link between expert performance and focused practice. Both conclude that mastering any domain comes down to one thing and one thing only: the number of hours spent in *deliberate practice*. Interestingly, due to biological limits, even top performers can only spend about five hours a day in deliberate practice. Some of the aspects of deliberate practice include performing an activity perfectly (exactly as you would when it counts), repeating the activity an unthinkable number of times, having access to advanced instruction, and constantly pushing past your current comfort levels. The problem for many people is that once they become good at something, they lose their motivation to become great at it. This is due to the plateau effect,[4] which causes people to make rapid gains early in their pursuit of mastery and then level off once they have become proficient, or moderately successful.

The 10,000-hour rule should be acknowledged, not followed. While there's no way to get around the fact

The key is to increase the quality of each hour that you spend in deliberate practice.

that you will have to consistently apply yourself to achieve greatness in any area of your life, there are a handful of things you can do to shave hours from the rule. The key is to increase the quality of each hour that you spend in deliberate practice. There are six different ways to do this: association, convergence, metamorphosis, ritualization, automation, and adjustment.

Association

Association can help you double, triple, or quadruple the quality of each hour you spend in deliberate practice. You are the average of the half-dozen people you hang out with the most. Start boosting your average by creating small tribes or mastermind groups that enhance your perspective, keep you focused, and inspire you.

In *Tribes*, author Seth Godin defines a tribe as a group of people connected to one another and connected to an idea.[5] A small group needs only two things to be a tribe: a shared interest and a way to communicate. For a long time I was convinced the only way to achieve mastery was to work long and hard all on my own. I thought this was the quickest way to perfect a skill and get ahead. Only when I started working with small teams of scientists for my passion projects after graduate school did I learn the value of creating tribes. I've now formed three different mastermind groups: one relating to my scientific pursuits, one relating to my goals as a writer and blogger, and one relating to goals in marketing and business.

If you're the smartest person in your group, it's time to get some new members. In the book *Mastery*, Robert Greene tells how Albert Einstein graduated from Zurich Polytechnic in 1900 without any job prospects.[6] He had graduated near the bottom of the class, giving him little to no chance of obtaining a teaching position. In 1902, after working in a patent office for two years, Einstein formed "The Olympia Academy" with two friends, who met to discuss books about science and philosophy. Three years later, Einstein's *Annus Mirabilis* papers vaulted him to international fame.

Think of the individuals in your tribe as people to share hours with. Every hour you spend taking purposeful action with two other focused people equals three total hours towards your 10,000-hour rule. The key is to form a tribe with people who push you outside of your comfort zone and, most importantly, have strengths and perspectives that you lack.

Convergence

Converge your efforts so that everything you do brings you closer to mastering your chosen pursuits. I've decided that I want to achieve mastery in three areas: science, writing, and public speaking. I'm coming to terms with the fact this is going to take me another five to ten years of deliberate practice. For example, over the last two years, I've given about 230 different two- to four-hour live presentations. If we average the length of those presentations to three hours and multiply those hours by 230, I've accumulated 690 hours of deliberate practice in the area of professional public speaking. Even at my current pace, which is about 38 hours of deliberate practice per month, I need another 245 months, or 20 years, of public speaking to achieve mastery. And that's assuming I stay fully engaged and continue to push past my limits for each of those hours.

What about my other interests? How can I reach the 10,000-hour mark in the realm of science and writing if it's going to take me 20 years to reach that same mark in public speaking? The answer is *convergence*: overlapping your pursuits to increase the quality of your hours. The only way for me to become a truly great scientist, writer, and public speaker, this side of 50 years old, is to converge my interests.

For example, if I'm speaking to a group of people about a science-related subject for two hours, those hours count towards both my pursuit of mastery in science and my pursuit of mastery in public speaking. Likewise, if I spend 15 hours writing, practicing, and revising scripts for a blog video, those hours count towards becoming a great writer and speaker. The key is being more flexible in the processes you use to achieve mastery. Start seeing everything you do as an opportunity to add hours of deliberate practice.

Metamorphosis

Stand on the deliberate practice of others through the process of *metamorphosis*. Insisting on starting from scratch instead of spring boarding off the ideas of others is a recipe for mediocrity. If you want to achieve mastery, stop trying to reinvent the wheel. For example, creative writing instructors will often ask their new students to take a poem or paragraph from an established author and reconstruct the author's message using their own words. Likewise, a classic non-fiction writing exercise is to read a bestselling book and summarize the author's message in a single page. As their skill matures, the students start creating their own original work. However, they forever maintain the influence of those who inspired them.

Don't be afraid to take hours from other people. Creativity is simply the practice of connecting things you already know in new ways. The key is that you can't connect things you don't know exist. This is where reading, knowledge, and building references come into play. The hard truth is, you will never achieve mastery by starting at the bottom. There's just not enough time in one life. Start increasing the quality of your hours by increasing your knowledge base. Learn everything you can about your chosen pursuit and then transform the work of others into your own. Once you've connected things in a new way, it's yours. Give credit to your influences and provide proper references, but don't be scared to rework and build on the ideas of others.

> **The hard truth is, you will never achieve mastery by starting at the bottom. There's just not enough time in one life.**

Ritualization

Ritualization is the process of creating rituals, or habits. In the book *The Power of Habit*, Charles Duhigg discusses a study involving mice in a cheese maze.[7] The first time the mice were put into a particular maze, their brain activity was robust and intense. The mice sniffed and clawed the walls, analyzing every part of the maze as they raced through it to find the cheese at the end. Here's the interesting part: if the mice were put in the same maze day and after day, they found the cheese faster, but their overall brain activity decreased. The mice had ritualized the process of finding the cheese. They'd formed a habit. During ritualization, a tiny part of your brain, called the *basal ganglia*, takes over a series of actions so that you no longer have to actively concentrate or make decisions. In this way, your brain conserves mental energy.

The first time the mice were put into a particular maze, their brain activity was robust and intense.

Ritualization saves willpower. Ritualization is what allows you to tie your shoe or brush your teeth without thinking about it. The rituals rely on triggers, routines, and rewards. The more rituals you can build *around* your hours of deliberate practice, the more mental energy you will have available for those hours.

Automation

Start automating as much of your life as possible. *Automation* is the process of using people, machines, and control systems to perform tasks that do not require your direct engagement. You can conserve willpower and increase the quality of the hours you spend in deliberate practice by having other people take care of your daily tasks.

Automation differs from ritualization in that it doesn't involve any direct action by you. Instead of putting your own actions on autopilot, other entities perform the action for you. I am a big fan of hiring virtual assistants and specialized freelance workers to take care of my administrative tasks. Of course, it's important for you to spend the proper amount of time training these assistants to perform their tasks properly; otherwise, they can cause mistakes that will detract from the quality of your hours.

Finally, you cannot automate your interactions with other people. Connecting with others will always require your own direct, focused engagement. A lot of businesses learn this lesson the hard way by trying to outsource their customer support, only to find they lose a lot of their best customers.

Adjustment

Adjustment is the process of restructuring your internal and external environments to increase the quality of your deliberate practice hours. Experiments at Florida State University found that the ability to successfully use willpower for self-control is dependent on physiological factors, most notably your blood glucose levels.[8]

Decisions involving willpower deplete your blood glucose stores and when these stores run low, you have a hard time using willpower to inhibit your behavior. This is why you have the urge to binge or make belligerent decisions late at night or after a long week of work. The key here is to make your body less reliant on blood glucose by restricting your carbohydrate intake and eating a diet consisting mostly of plants and animals. The less your insulin levels fluctuate, the less your willpower fluctuates.

Your external environment can crush your hopes and dreams.

Control your environment or it will control you. Your external environment can crush your hopes and dreams. If you have a sweet tooth and are trying to lose weight, don't keep a box of Twinkies in your house. It's much easier to say no to a Twinkie if you never see one—out of sight, out of mind. By keeping temptations and negative influences out of sight, you take away the need to make a good decision. As a result, you save your decision-making units for deliberate hours of practice.

Similarly, if your goal is to work out every morning, start laying out your gym clothes the night before. That way, you take away the decision of what to wear and what to do when you wake up. Restructure your environment so that it fits with your pursuit of mastery. Align every part of your life with your overall purpose in life.

26

Avoid the Life Hack Lie

"Short cuts make for long delays."

J.R.R. Tolkien

When did life hacking turn into hedonism? When did Burning Man[9] turn into Mount Sinai?[10] Life hacking is a dirty lie being told worldwide. Stuffing your brain with how-to lists and executing get-rich-quick schemes will not fulfill you. Neither will partying at some festival or traveling around the world without a reason. WHY? Your soul needs more. There are no shortcuts to greatness or fulfillment. Sure, you can read a four-step guide on swinging a golf club better, but those tips won't turn you into Tiger Woods overnight. You have to take action in the real world by swinging a driver millions of times for ten to twenty years. Of course, trying different activities, or hacking life, can help you *find* your purpose. But there's no way to get around the fact that you will have to pay your dues for years to *fulfill* a worthy purpose.

Becoming truly great doesn't come easy

Shortcuts are addictive. I am a recovering life hack addict. The first year after I graduated with my PhD, I started a professional development blog,[11] launched two online products, worked full-time as an Application Scientist, consulted for several companies, and gave hundreds of seminars around the world. I love the idea of being a jack-of-all-trades, shaking my life up, mass-executing different ventures, and becoming an expert overnight. These things are appealing because they seem to infuse your life with freedom, mobility, and constant change. On the other hand, grinding out mastery in one or two areas hurts.

Becoming truly great in a field requires massive action in a single direction for years.

One of the keys to mastery is staying committed to principles while staying unattached to processes.

In the book *The Dip*,[12] Seth Godin explains how smart people can tell the difference between a cul-de-sac (French for "dead end") and a dip. A cul-de-sac is a situation where you work and work and work, and nothing much changes. A dip, like a plateau, is the lull that occurs after an initial period of growth on your way to fulfilling your purpose. Don't give up on your dips. Dedication, tenacity, failing repeatedly, and leaning into "the dip" can be painful. Greatness doesn't come easy; it requires commitment. And that's a good thing. The whole point of mastery is to rise above mediocre knowledge and achievement. If that were easy to do, everyone would do it. Becoming truly great in a field requires massive action in a single direction for years.

Don't confuse flakiness with flexibility

To achieve mastery, you have to rely on the same proven principles that have carried people to greatness for centuries. Certain principles are constant, like having integrity, maintaining a disciplined work ethic, building strong relationships, and staying focused on adding value over making money. On the other hand, most processes change with the times, like using manufacturing assembly lines, recording on eight-track tapes, and printing the news on paper. One of the keys to mastery is staying committed to principles while staying unattached to processes. In other words, be flexible but not flaky. Flexibility is a principle. In order to fulfill your purpose in life, you will have to be flexible in whatever processes serve you best. At the same time, you will have to stay dedicated to tried-and-true principles; otherwise, you're just a flake.

The problem with life hacking is that it encourages flakiness, promising to help people achieve mastery in a dozen different areas in six months or less. The dirty secret is that the people promoting a life hacking lifestyle are diligently working their butts off behind the scenes to achieve mastery in the fields of writing, speaking, marketing, and selling.

27

Avoid Willpower Depletion

"Nothing can withstand the power of the human will if it is willing to stake its very existence to the extent of its purpose."

Benjamin Disraeli

Reserve your willpower for your pursuit of mastery. One of the best pieces of advice I ever received in graduate school came from one of my committee members. I was struggling to write my thesis. Specifically, I was having a hard time producing more than a paragraph or two a day. I would write sporadically whenever I had time between experiments, or I would write late at night after I got home from a long day in the lab.

After I told him how I was writing, he shook his head and said, "Here's what you do: first thing in the morning, right after you wake up and eat breakfast, take your computer and your notes to the science library, lock yourself in one of the study rooms, write for five hours, and be done. Don't write any more after that because it will all be crap. Do that every day in the exact same way and you'll be finished in two weeks."

I thought he was nuts. There's no way I could finish my thesis in two weeks, especially after hearing countless stories of other students taking six months to a year to finish their theses. But I gave it a shot. I finished my entire thesis in 13 days. Without knowing it at the time, I had utilized the key principles of deliberate practice and the five-hour rule to be massively productive.

Willpower depletion theory

Willpower depletion theory is the idea that the human mind has a limited reserve of willpower. "Willpower" is defined as the ability to control your own behavior. It can be thought of as a kind of

Deliberate practice relies on willpower. And your willpower consists of a set number of decision-making units.

instinctual override; a way to interrupt your brain's automatic processing in order to do something else.

For example, if you're hungry and come upon a table of free doughnuts, the primitive part of your brain will process the event and say, "EAT!" But the more advanced decision-making part of your brain will tell you to keep walking and not take the bait. Willpower is simply your ability to inhibit your brain's natural inclinations. In other words, willpower is your ability to make good decisions.

Cognitive strain inhibits willpower

Studies have shown that each person has his or her own individual willpower limit, and this limit is depleted by mental effort. In the book *How We Decide*, Jonah Lehrer discusses an experiment performed by professor Baba Shiv at Stanford University.[13] The experiment involved two groups of students: individuals in the first group were given a two-digit number to remember, while individuals in the second group were given a seven-digit number to remember. Both groups were instructed to remember the number, walk down a long hallway, and repeat the number to an administrator at the end of the hall. Halfway down the hall, a young woman waited by a table with a large plate of fresh fruit on one side and a large plate of pastries on the other side. She asked each participant to choose which snack they would like to eat after completing the memorization task. The people in the second group—those laboring under the strain of remembering a seven-digit number—chose a pastry far more often than those who were remembering the two-digit number.

Deliberate practice relies on willpower. And your willpower consists of a set number of decision-making units. These units affect your ability not only to make good decisions, but to focus and concentrate in general. Regardless of whether or not you can increase your willpower, the amount of mental strain you can put yourself through each day is limited. Once you reach your personal limit, you will lose your ability to concentrate and make good decisions.

By definition, deliberate practice requires a person to be completely engaged in a task, to repeat the task over and over, and to receive and respond to immediate feedback. This kind of effort requires constant decision-making. The practicing person has to continually make decisions to stay engaged, respond to feedback, and figure out how to proceed. As a result, deliberate practice results in a high level of mental strain. This is why even top performers only spend five hours a day in deliberate practice. Due to willpower depletion, any time spent practicing beyond this number is not worth the investment.

Once you reach your personal limit, you will lose your ability to concentrate and make good decisions.

Case Study

Matt Giulianelli, DMD

Matt Giulianelli, DMD, flew through his first two years of dental school at Tufts University. He received high marks in almost all of his classes and got along really well with his classmates. Going into his third year, Matt was ready (and excited) to see patients. During the first few weeks of clinic, Matt and his classmates shadowed faculty members performing difficult dental procedures. As Matt watched these procedures, he was blown away by how small a space the dentists had to operate in. Yes, he knew that a person's mouth was small, and that an individual tooth was even smaller—but he didn't know that 500 micrometers could be the difference between a successful procedure and a disaster. A micrometer, or micron, is 1,000 times smaller than a millimeter, which is over 25 times smaller than an inch. Given the significance of these tiny distances, dentists fill cavities and perform other dental procedures with the aid of surgical telescopic eyewear called *loupes* that magnify a person's mouth by 2.5 to six times. But even with these magnification capabilities, a dentist's fine motor skills are crucial to his or her success.

It wasn't inches that mattered; it was microns. If Matt wanted to be a successful dentist, he would have to develop and master his fine motor skills quickly. The only problem was that mastering any skill required 10,000 hours of deliberate practice. Of course, his professors discussed fine motor skills with Matt in class, and he had even been tested on these skills. But he completely lacked any real world experience. Matt was starting from scratch; or, put another way, he was starting at zero hours of deliberate practice.

Just a couple of years after residency, Matt made the conscious decision to become a master in his field. Matt acknowledged the 10,000 hour rule. However, he also knew he could break this rule by making a handful of key changes.

He was going to have to create some new *rituals*, *adjust* his internal and external environment and *automate* his focus. For Matt, exercising had always been important. He would go to the gym at different times, whenever he could fit it in. But Matt's random gym schedule required him to make several decisions, like when and how to get his workout gear, when and how to get to the gym, and what exercises to do when he got there. As a result, his willpower suffered. On days when Matt decided to go to the gym, he would have no energy left in the evening to study and practice his fine motor skills.

Matt made going to the gym a habit. Instead of randomly choosing to go to the gym here and there, he started going to the gym every morning, right after eating breakfast and brushing his teeth. Eventually, Matt *ritualized* this morning routine. By stacking his new habit onto these other longstanding habits, Matt was able to conserve a significant amount of mental energy. Matt also kept his internal and external environment in check by stocking his fridge and cabinets with healthy food only. By *adjusting* his environment, he always ate a nutritious breakfast.

Matt also started *automating* time by delegating tasks to team members at the office so that he could spend more time with patients in deliberate practice during the day. Once he was able to train them to perform certain procedures (within their scope of practice), he found that he could spend more time with his patients and see more patients during the day.

Matt squeezed every drop from his hours of deliberate practice. He was successfully preventing willpower depletion through adjustment, automation, and ritualization. But this wasn't enough. Matt wanted to achieve mastery even faster.

The first thing Matt did was to start watching videos and attending courses that featured masters who were renowned in the field of dentistry. Matt watched these masters perform procedures, mimicking their hand movements until their techniques became his techniques. In other words, he *metamorphosized* the masters' techniques. In a few short years, Matt watched hundreds of training videos and attended close to 100 hours of continuing education courses. The average dentist only attends 20.

Next, Matt joined a consulting network, or mastermind group, of like-minded dentists. During their group meetings, Matt and the other members discussed innovations in the industry and showed each other cutting-edge techniques, many of which helped them improve their fine motor skills. Through the process of *association*, all of the members of the group were able to exponentially improve their procedures and create better outcomes for their patients. Finally, Matt *converged* his efforts. Any time he saw patients or learned new dental processes and procedures, he would simultaneously practice his fine motor skills. Any time he was at the gym, or at home washing dishes, or flipping through the pages of a textbook, Matt focused on improving his fine motor skills.

Matt obliterated the 10,000 hour rule. After graduating from Tufts, Matt was invited to stay in Boston and complete a hospital-based General Practice Residency at Boston Medical Center. In 2011, he was awarded Fellowship in the Academy of General Dentistry, a distinction that only 3% of dentists in North America earn. Currently, Matt and his wife run a private practice in Vermont and Matt routinely reviews journal articles for the Academy of General Dentistry.[14]

Looking back at his path to mastery, Matt recalls the words a world-renowned dentist said to him during a continuing education course: "Practice doesn't make perfect, perfect practice makes perfect."

28

Develop a Can-Do Mindset

"The winners in life think constantly in terms of I can, I will, and I am. Losers, on the other hand, concentrate their waking thoughts on what they should have or would have done, or what they can't do."

Denis Waitley

One day, in graduate school, my mentor walked over to my lab bench and looked down at me while I pipetted cells into a test tube.

"What do you think about doing a set of proliferation assays on your cells?" he said.

"Great, let's do it," I replied.

"No, no, slow down—I asked you what you *thought* about it."

Confused, I said, "I *think* it's a great idea, let's do it. I'll set up the assay today."

"A can-do attitude doesn't fit in academia. I want you to start being more reserved."

This is the kind of advice I received throughout graduate school. Calm down. Slow down. Sit down. Tone yourself down. Ask permission. Follow directions. These bland, soul-sucking slogans will shrink your self-confidence and erode your motivation.

Most organizations (and people for that matter) preach obligation, passivity, and reliance on the herd. They want you to spend life coloring within the lines, playing it safe, and trying to make everyone happy. People who have this mindset will indeed move forward—like lemmings over a cliff. The only way to reach your mountaintop is to develop a can-do mindset. A can-do mindset is one of bold, creative action. Someone with a can-do attitude is positive, a go-getter, upbeat, confident, keen, self-reliant, and ambitious. A can-do person runs towards obstacles, enjoying each challenge and learning from each failure. Most importantly, a can-do person takes initiative. When there is no way, these people make a way. They have a bias for action. This kind of mental outlook is required to fulfill your purpose in life.

Compulsive planners finish last

Some of the brightest and most successful people in business, including recent MBA graduates and Fortune 500 CEOs, have tried the Marshmallow Challenge.[15] This is how the test works: people are divided into teams of four. Each team is given 20 sticks of precooked (hard) spaghetti, a yard of tape, a yard of string, and one marshmallow. Each team is then given 18 minutes to build the tallest structure they can—but, the marshmallow must be on top. The challenge was created by designer Peter Skillman and it has since been used by innovation expert Tom Wujec to evaluate how executives collaborate and innovate. The results are surprising. The worst performing groups of people include recent MBA graduates, with CEOs of large organizations being only slightly better. One of the top performing groups of people are kindergarteners.

No plan survives contact with reality.

In *Stop Talking, Start Doing*,[16] Shaa Wasmund reveals that the reason kindergarteners succeed while their older, more educated rivals fail is kindergarteners' bias for action. The MBA grads planned, postured, assigned roles and responsibilities, and then, as time ran out, scrambled to build a tower of spaghetti and place a marshmallow on top, only to watch everything crumble under the weight of the marshmallow at the last minute. Meanwhile, the kindergarteners, being kids, just took action. They started building right from the start and quickly found what worked and what didn't. They didn't worry about failing. They didn't hesitate. They just took action.

No plan survives contact with reality. Reading books and writing plans are great ways to build references, maintain focus, and enhance perspective—but experience is the best and fastest teacher. Experience requires action, and action requires visceral contact with reality. The only way to keep your life aligned with your new purpose is to maintain a sense of urgency and action.

Patience is a vice

Prolonged study, deliberation, and planning are often signs of weakness and insecurity, not wisdom and patience. Planning is safe, which is why most people set it as their default state. Plans are cheap. Experience is costly. Taking action in the real world involves risk, which is why most people procrastinate obsessively.

Prolonged study, deliberation, and planning are often signs of weakness and insecurity, not wisdom and patience.

Waiting for the right moment or the right person is foolish. No one is coming to pave you a safe path to success. No one is going to magically appear and pick you for greatness. Fairy godmothers don't exist. Stop waiting. Pick yourself. Make something happen right now. Be your own big break.

29

Think Inside the Box and Move Laterally

"It is a narrow mind which cannot look at a subject from various points of view."

George Eliot

The biggest lesson I've learned in the past two years is that you can get a lot done by thinking inside the box, moving laterally, and building your dreams around your current position in life.

Realize you are the box

When I started blogging and creating online products, I felt like a phony. I felt like I needed to be someone else. The problem was I was looking vertically and trying to think outside the box. One day, I realized that the box I was trying to climb out of was myself. Everything changed once I started seeing myself as the person I wanted to be "right now," using the things I already had at my disposal to initiate change. I stopped trying to replicate the mythical images of a successful person I had in my head. Instead, I started expressing myself authentically and building my pursuits around my biggest strengths. I also started looking at the relationships I already had to get things done instead of trying to make some perfect connection.

Resourcefulness is the ability to use what you already have to get what you want. Self-reliance means you can count on yourself, or who you are right now, to fulfill your purpose. This includes investing in your current relationships rather than looking for someone new to hold your hand.

Turn your focus inward and sideways

In the past, when I was gearing up to launch a new project, the first questions I asked were, "What do I need to get this done in the future?" and "Who can I find to do this for me?" Now, when I start a new project, I ask myself, "What do I already have that will help me get this done right now?" and "Who do I already know who can do this with me?" This simple shift in my perspective completely changed my life. The quickest way to change your focus is to change the questions that you are asking yourself. Changing my questions shifted my perspective from outside and vertical to inside and lateral.

First, I started seeing the value in what I already had. Instead of immediately assuming I needed something new or needed to meet someone new, I started assuming I already had everything I needed. Second, I took action towards new goals immediately. Instead of assuming I wouldn't have the necessary tools until a later point, I assumed I had everything I needed right now. Third, I saw my relationships as opportunities for collaboration. Instead of assuming people were only interested in having work outsourced to them, I assumed they were interested in building something together.

You are in control of your focus

If you're only focused on what you don't have, you'll only see what you don't have. This limited mindset will keep you from coming up with creative ways to use your current talents and your current connections. Shifting your focus to what you already have and maintaining an *abundance mentality* is the only way to keep moving toward your purpose in the face of adversity.

If you're only focused on what you don't have, you'll only see what you don't have.

No matter what you're up against, whether it's a difficult circumstance, negative person, or your own negative emotions, you get to choose your focus. Choosing your focus can put you in a positive state. It can also help you give your obstacles a positive meaning, and show you how to use your obstacles to your advantage. The more you are in control of your focus, the more you are in control of your purpose.

30

Manipulate Reality

....

"What we see depends mainly on what we look for."

John Lubbock

Perspective moves your focus. Your perspective is built on your references and belief system. The more references you have, the broader your perspective. A far-reaching knowledge base and a flexible belief system will help you see more opportunities. The key is to grow your references with useful knowledge rather than useless information, and bend your belief system without sacrificing your principles. Your aim is to believe anything is possible, while recognizing not everything should be realized.

Recall, in Chapter 5, that most people are able to run faster during the last sprint of a workout than during the second-to-last sprint. Why? Because after their coaches yell, "Last one, give everything" their perspectives change. The sprinters go from having an undetermined number of sprints to perform to having a clear and concise number of sprints to perform. As a result, their bodies are immediately infused with more energy. Perspective is the key to the equation: *purpose equals hope equals energy.*

Be flexible in your process and perspective

Supreme flexibility in perspective and process is the trade secret of successful people. In particular, your ability to tamper with your own viewpoint will help you fulfill your purpose. Most people maintain a very limited perspective. Either they have convinced themselves they lack what's needed to be successful, or they simply do not believe they are capable of being successful. On the other hand, some people have an extremely broad perspective but have lost the ability to focus. These people remain lost in a sea of options and are often overwhelmed by life's possibilities. Maintaining your new direction in life relies on your ability to shift your focus and perspective at will.

Attack your perspective

Try the following exercises:[17] first, stop reading, close your eyes, and for ten seconds think of as many WHITE objects as possible. Once you open your eyes, immediately write down the number of items that came to your mind. Now, do the same thing, except this time, think of as many WHITE objects in your refrigerator as possible. After ten seconds, write down the number of items that came to your mind. If you're like most people, you were able to think of more things the second time. Why? Because limiting your answers to objects found in a refrigerator limited your focus. When your focus was unlimited, your mind wasn't able to focus.

> Maintaining your new direction in life relies on your ability to shift your focus and perspective at will.

For the next exercise,[18] stop reading and look around the room you're in and find everything RED that you can see. Take a mental note of every RED item in the room. RED, RED, RED. Remember these items so you can write them down. GO. Now, get a piece of paper and, without looking around anymore, write down as many green items in the room that you can remember.

If you followed the above directions, odds are you could only think of one or two green items, if any. This is how your perspective can affect your focus and vice versa. If your perspective is too limited, you can completely miss what's right in front of you. If your perspective is unlimited, you can freeze up and fail to focus on anything. In order to fulfill your purpose, you have to be able to actively zoom in and out of any part of your life at any time.

Differentiate knowledge from useless information

Your reticular activating system is like cookies for your brain. A computer cookie,[19] also known as a Web, browser, or HTTP cookie, is a small piece of data sent from a website and stored in a user's Web browser while he or she is on the Internet. When the user browses the same website in the future, the data stored in the cookie is retrieved by the website to notify the website of the user's previous activity. Cookies were designed to help websites recall activities that the user has performed in the past. Cookies focus your computer on the most important information from your previous browsing experiences.

You can manipulate reality by building references and playing with your perspective.

Similarly, your brain's reticular activating system focuses you on the most important information from your past life experiences. The reticular activating system is a set of connected nuclei that help regulate attention in the brains of vertebrates. During tasks that require increased alertness and attention, there is increased blood flow in this formation. Your reticular activating system is what helps you store and recall references.

Experience is the best reference. Have you ever noticed something for the first time, like a certain type of car, and then started to see that car everywhere? It's not that sales of this particular car suddenly spiked; it's that your reticular activating system logged this car into your brain. This car is now a highlighted reference.[20] It's part of your awareness. The key is to use your reticular activating system discerningly to increase your number of productive references. Don't waste this system on reality television, gossip magazines, and 24-hour news commentary. Be selective. Read and watch things that are going to bring you closer to fulfilling your purpose in life.

The only way to fulfill your purpose in life is to continually build references related to your purpose. The best way to build references is to engage your reticular activating system. And the best way to engage your reticular activating system is to take action. Actions create experiences. Experiences create references.

You can manipulate reality by building references and playing with your perspective. If you are feeling uninspired and find yourself procrastinating on a project, inject yourself with a sense of urgency by setting an aggressive deadline, telling everyone about it, and focusing on how your reputation will be damaged if you fail to meet it. If you are overly stressed about a deadline and it's affecting your productivity, shift your perspective by looking to a bigger picture. Missing one deadline never ruined anyone's career forever.

Manipulate reality, but don't abandon it. Acknowledge past mistakes and failures, and allow for the fact that there will be more in the future. Even negative experiences can create productive references that expand your perspective.

31

Build Rome Around Your Safety Net

> *"You can have anything you want if you are willing to give up the belief that you can't have it."*
>
> Robert Anthony

Working without a safety net is overrated. You don't have to give up your day job to fulfill your purpose. Over the last few years, dozens of books, blogs, and businesses have promoted the idea that you need to "fire your boss" in order to fulfill your dreams. As a result, many people think they can't be successful in life until they give up their jobs. This perspective is extremely limiting.

Keep your job as a safety net

In today's world, many businesses promote a can-do mindset. Men and women of action who start their own projects now get promoted faster and are given more freedom in the workplace. The best known example of this is Google's 20% rule.[21] Google allows its engineers to spend 20% of their time on projects that directly interest them. These engineers are paid to spend an entire day's worth of company time working on whatever they want. Hit products including Gmail and Google News were created through this 20% program. Just as a company can build on your interests, you can build on your company's interests. Start seeing your job as a means of maintaining your new direction. Keep your job as a safety net and build your interests around it.

Do it all. Have a whatever-it-takes mentality. Throw as many things against the wall as possible. You can always narrow your focus later. In other words, limit your goals, not the ways in which you can accomplish them. Keep your mountain peak stationary, but keep your route to the summit flexible. Most people set a goal and then restrict themselves to one set way of accomplishing it. This mindset is absurd.

Limiting beliefs are the only things stopping you from fulfilling your purpose without giving up anything good. If your goal is to travel abroad and help sick children, don't refuse an opportunity to volunteer at a hospital in India just because you saw yourself volunteering in Indonesia. Go to Indonesia next time. Limiting beliefs are the only things stopping you from fulfilling your purpose without giving up anything good. Learn to ignore ultimatums and decisions that involve the word "or." Never limit your options without first trying to change the word "or" to "and."

Your perspective is based on your belief system. If you believe there is only one way to achieve your goal, then you limit yourself to that one option. However, if you believe there are a thousand different ways to achieve your goal, then you have a thousand different options. This is why it is important to stay flexible in your perspective and processes. Set your principles in stone, not your processes. When forced to decide between two things, choose both. In other words, keep your safety nets. Give up nothing. Do everything.

Case Study

Michael Smith, MBA

Michael wanted to make something happen for himself. Sure, he had excelled in his career and made good business decisions, and, as a result, was promoted rapidly. Michael worked in sales management at Vygon,[22] a large European medical device company, and later at Johnson & Johnson.[23] Yet, despite his success, he always felt like he was just doing what he was told. He felt like he was following the lead of others.

Now Michael wanted to open his own door. He wanted to have his own business and he wanted to be his own boss. He wanted to initiate something. In particular, Michael wanted to be an author and a private sales coach; but he didn't want to give up his job to make this happen.

Michael changed his life by making a decision to do something no one had told him to do: enroll in the Warwick Business School's MBA program.[24] Michael quickly completed his degree while working full-time in his current sales and marketing position. Then, without being told to, Michael signed up for Henley Business School's Executive Coaching program,[25] again, while working full-time in his sales position. Soon, Michael was addicted to initiating action. Instead of waiting for permission to do things, he started picking himself. He developed a can-do mindset. And, he started to build Rome around his safety net.

Recently, Michael launched his new company, brand, and blog called "Go Naked: Revealing the Secrets of Powerful Relationships."[26] At the same time, he took on an even more senior role for a large multinational company. Currently, Michael is the Director of European Sales for Align Technology. He is also a successful sales coach and author. He published his first book under the Go Naked banner in early 2014.

32

Generate Me Capital

....

"If a man empties his purse into his head, no one can take it from him. An investment in knowledge always pays the highest return."

Benjamin Franklin

All growth is a consequence of good investment. Chapters 28–31 of this book discussed the importance of having a can-do attitude, acting before you are ready, being flexible, and managing your perspective. The next step to maintaining your new direction in life is to consistently invest in yourself and other people. Adding value to your life and the lives of others will add value to your purpose. It will also help you see more opportunities.

When I was a kid growing up in northern Idaho, my dad often drove me past Silverwood Theme Park. It's located off Highway 95, the only highway in and out of town. Every time we drove past Silverwood, there seemed to be a new ride to look at. When I first saw the park, there was one rollercoaster, a Ferris wheel, and a log flume ride. A year later, there was another, larger rollercoaster. Then there was a bumper boat ride, then another Ferris wheel, and then a third rollercoaster. Recently the owner added an entire waterpark, including a wave pool and several large waterslides. Silverwood continues to grow and is now the Pacific Northwest's largest amusement park.[27] What was the owner doing all of these years? He was investing in himself.

You are your own best investment

Spend your time, money, and energy taking care of your most valuable asset: you. If you're a mess mentally or physically, you can't build strong relationships or put a dent in the universe. In order to consistently add value to other people and projects, you have to consistently add value to yourself. Research and development, or

Spend your time, money, and energy taking care of your most valuable asset: you. If you're a mess mentally or physically, you can't build strong relationships or put a dent in the universe.

R&D, is what large corporations rely on to determine what they should do next. Some businesses spend millions, or even billions, of dollars every year on speculative research meant to stimulate growth and spur innovation.

Company R&D is valuable because it keeps a company on the cutting edge of its field. Similarly, self-R&D is valuable because it keeps you on the cutting edge of your pursuits, pushing you to take ground towards your biggest goals. Start beefing up your self-R&D division. You can do this by attending conferences, taking online courses, or investing in non-fiction books related to your new purpose. In *The Personal MBA*, author Josh Kaufman suggests starting a self-R&D fund by allocating 5% of your monthly income to personal development and lifestyle experimentation.[28] The best way to add value to your life is by learning as much as possible, and by having as many productive experiences as possible. Make knowledge and action your most valuable assets.

33

Invest in People, Not Ideas

"You will get all you want in life if you help enough other people get what they want."

Zig Ziglar

You can't automate human interactions. When I first started working online, I would find a new contractor on Elance[29] or some other freelance website every time I had a new project. This was not only unproductive but was unfulfilling. Using a different contractor for every new project meant starting and ending a new relationship with every project. This meant, for each project, I had to sift through and interview dozens of freelance artists, choose one, explain to him or her not only what I wanted done but how I wanted it done, and then work with that freelancer, through trial and error, to close the project.

One day, I realized that it would be far more efficient and meaningful to develop a long-term relationship with a few key contractors. First, I started going back to the same Web development team, who I originally met on Elance, for all of my programming projects. Next, I developed a long-term relationship with a graphic design artist who I initially hired as a one-project contractor. Finally, I found someone who I already knew to start doing all of my video work. Now, when I'm ready to start a new project, I have a team of people who know exactly how I like things done.

Building strong relationships is strategic, not tactical

Strategy involves long-term thinking and long-term investment. This means treating your relationships as an end in themselves, rather than as a short-term, or tactical, means to getting something else. What you are really investing in is people, not projects.

You can't outsource your health or relationships. Maintaining your new direction in life involves learning to work with yourself and others effectively. No one can build an empire without staying healthy, both mentally and physically, and without building strong relationships. Great ideas are useless without great people behind them. Human interaction is the only thing that can turn a dream into reality. Your project can't close itself. Your product can't buy itself. You need people. You need connections.

You can't outsource your health or relationships.

34

Connect Without Getting Lost in the Crowd

"Your network is your net worth."

John C. Maxwell

Successful networking is a combination of creating deep connections and differentiating yourself from these connections. Connection is the only way to bring ideas, actions, and people together. Without connection, everything would stay the same. But connection comes with a price. The more you connect, the more you dilute your identity. The only way to keep yourself from getting lost in the crowd is to hold up a very distinctive flag. This flag, or brand, is a symbol of who you are and what you're about. The key is creating a flag that is both recognizable and memorable. And the best way to do this is by combining familiar reference points in unfamiliar ways.

First, you have create a network of deep connections. Next, you have to differentiate yourself from these connections. Otherwise, you and your purpose will get buried in your surroundings. A strong sense of who you are, backed by a unique yet relatable message, will help you connect without getting lost in the crowd.

"I would rather have 1,000 friends than 1,000 dollars." This is what a friend of mine used to say to me over and over again in college. What a bunch of garbage, I thought. Give me the money. I can do everything on my own. I don't have time to sit around, nurture relationships, or talk about my feelings. I have goals to achieve.

Connection is a crutch—that was my slogan. As a result, I went through most of college and graduate school careers focusing entirely on myself and my work. This approach moved me forward, for a while. But then I started getting stuck. Every few months, I would end up chasing my tail or hitting a dead end. I had trouble

It's hard to look ahead when your nose is glued to the grindstone.

figuring out what to do next and it seemed like I was always the last to know about new opportunities. It's hard to look ahead when your nose is glued to the grindstone. Eventually, I realized that connecting with other people is just as important to my progress as my individual work ethic.

Soft skills nurture hard skills

A study published by the *Academy of Management Journal*[30] concluded that successful managers spend 70% more time networking than their less successful counterparts. Other studies have shown that networking in business and entrepreneurship circles is positively associated with salary growth, number of promotions, perceived career success, and job satisfaction.[31] The truth is that connections crush qualifications. Your experience, job title, resume, and skill sets are nothing compared to someone else's strong connections. Almost half of all job hires at top-tier companies are referrals. Referrals are also the number one source of hiring volume, quality, speed, and employment length. Yet referrals only make up 7% of all job applicants.[32] This means that the majority of the population is either not connecting enough or not using their connections effectively.

One connection can change your life forever

Have you ever met someone for the first time at a social event and, after five seconds, started looking over his or her shoulders for someone else to talk to? Stop it. Searching for *the next best person* is not networking. Most people make the mistake of thinking that connecting stops at getting a name card or a friend request. They rack up loose associations at the expense of engaging with anyone in particular. These people have been taught to value quantity over quality.

Don't skim your network. Instead, dig deeply into individual relationships. The dork with the glasses and the gum in their hair that keeps bothering you at the conference might be six months away from launching the next *Angie's List*.[33] In two years, the annoying person who responds to every single one of your Twitter updates might publish a book that influences your entire client base. The point is that every person you connect with is a human being, and all human beings have unlimited potential. The most important person in your network is the person whose attention you have right now. Don't obsess over saying "hello" to the biggest name in the room (or online) when you could be cutting a deal or creating something new with the "nobody" right in front of you.

> **Don't skim your network. Instead, dig deeply into individual relationships.**

Differentiate yourself in five seconds or less

Have you ever met a group of people for the first time at a social event and after five seconds watched their eyes drift over YOUR shoulders looking for someone else to talk to? It's your fault. You lost their interest. When you first meet someone, especially decision-makers at a networking event, you have a very short amount of time to get their attention. If you open a conversation with where you went to school or how the weather is, you're done. Eyes glazed. Attention lost. Game over.

A better strategy is to ask an engaging question and give the other person a chance to talk about themselves and their purpose. *Give* them your attention. The key word is *give*. Networking is not about getting something from other people, it's about giving yourself to other people. Don't sell yourself, don't act *better than*, and don't act like a fan. Treat everyone as your equal. Effective networking comes down to asking good questions and listening. It's as simple as that. And, when it's finally your turn to talk, have something interesting (and succinct) to say.

One minute of connecting equals fifty-five seconds of listening and five seconds of talking. But those last five seconds are crucial. This

One minute of connecting equals fifty-five seconds of listening and five seconds of talking. But those last five seconds are crucial.

is your time to describe yourself and your project in a way people will remember. Five seconds is all you have to show people that you're not just another resume, not just another businessman in a blue suit, and not just another entrepreneur in a graphic T-shirt. I've seen people wait all day to get in front of CEOs, book publishers, start-up giants, and other decision-makers, only to embarrass themselves when it's their turn to talk. What good is it to meet the founder and CEO of the *next big thing* if he won't remember your name or your idea two minutes later? (Or—worse—never want to see you again?)

35

Develop a Personalized Escalator Pitch

....

"If you can't explain it simply, you don't understand it well enough."

Albert Einstein

The best way to differentiate yourself from your network in a five-second time frame is by developing a personalized elevator pitch. An elevator pitch is a short statement used to define yourself, your profession, or your product, service, or idea, and its value proposition. A short trip on an elevator with someone is all the time you have to describe your idea in a way that gets the other person's attention. In fact, nowadays, you only have time to make an *escalator pitch*[34]—a pitch that lasts from the time it takes someone to cross your path going down an escalator while you're going up the opposite side. The leading way to do this is by comparing your brand to two other well-known reference points. The key is connecting these points in a unique and interesting way.

Differentiate yourself by connecting usual things in unusual ways. When I first started building my company, Cheeky Scientist,[35] I wasn't quite sure how to describe it to other people. I would say something about my experiences in graduate school, how I wanted to help people, what my natural talents were, blah, blah, blah. Now, I tell people that *Cheeky Scientist is Tony Robbins for nerds*. Most people in the personal development field know who Tony Robbins is and almost everyone has an idea of what a nerd is. I've also created the tagline *Personal Development for Intelligent People*. In both cases, I am connecting two concepts together in a way that helps differentiate who I am and what my project is about.

In the book *Microstyle*,[36] author Christopher Johnson calls this kind of differentiation a "high-concept pitch". Johnson writes that a high-concept pitch involves connecting existing reference points,

213

Differentiate yourself by connecting usual things in unusual ways.

such as another person, company, product, service, lifestyle, or object in a way that makes the idea seem familiar, yet unique, at the same time. A great example of this is the original pitch for the 1979 movie, *Alien*: "*Jaws* in space." They used *Jaws*, the world's most successful summer blockbuster movie, as the first well-known reference point and connected it to space, a second well-known reference point.[37] In three words, the producers were able to tap into everything their audience knew about the movie *Jaws* and everything they knew about space, while differentiating *Alien* from everything else they had ever seen. A high-concept pitch is an effective way to communicate your purpose. This kind of pitch will help you stand out without making other people bored or uncomfortable.

Building relationships is a strategy, not a tactic. The best way to network is by digging deep into your relationships while defining yourself in a unique and interesting way. Your goal is to connect without getting lost in the crowd. In the end, the bank can take away your house, car, and money, but it can't take away your relationships, your health, or your identity.

36

The Only Three Skills that Will Matter in Five Years

"Know that although in the eternal scheme of things you are small, you are also unique and irreplaceable, as are all your fellow humans everywhere in the world."

Margaret Laurence

Goodbye, information age—we are now in the idea age. An age, or era, dies once something better comes along that turns the valuable resource of the previous era into a commodity. The Stone Age was replaced by the Bronze Age, the Bronze Age was replaced by the Iron Age, and the information age has been replaced by the idea age. There used to be different degrees of accessibility to information. But now, thanks to the 24-hour news programs, the Internet, social media, cell phones, and a variety of other media channels and outlets, everyone has access. The world is completely saturated with information.

Ideas add quality to information

You create ideas from the best information. But things are moving fast. Just as we are entering the idea age, we are leaving it. Ideas are already commodities. In fact, there are idea farms—there is, in fact, a company actually called Ideafarms[38]—that will take in your raw idea and create a finished product, service, or company. There are websites, such as IdeaConnection,[39] that allow you to list and advertise your ideas so that interested investors and buyers can find them. It's like going to the grocery store, picking an idea off of the shelf, reading the label, and deciding whether or not you want to buy it. In a way, good ideas have always been commodities.

Everyone has at least one good idea. So what adds quality to an idea?

1 The ability to communicate it effectively.

2 The ability to take action and turn it into a physical reality.

3 The ability to choose the right idea in the first place.

Mastering each of these abilities, or skills, will help you achieve any goal. Your purpose will always be tied to oral communication, physical action, and mental choice. In the next decade, anything that doesn't require a significant amount of these three skills will quickly be replaced by a mobile app.

Improve oral communication

Oral communication is the first skill you should improve. If you go high enough up in any organization, the people at the top are the best oral communicators. This is because oral communication is the most direct way to share ideas, generate enthusiasm, and motivate others to action. Any business deal that involves more than a hot dog and a handshake requires at least one face-to-face meeting. Why? Because you can read a lot more into a person and a deal when things such as body language, mannerisms, facial expressions, and vocal tone come into play.

Your purpose will always be tied to oral communication, physical action, and mental choice.

Oral communication is the bottleneck through which all great ideas must pass. Despite all the rapid advances in technology, even top-of-the-line facial recognition software is faulty at best. Forget about a computer being able in the next 20 years to analyze rapidly changing facial expressions, along with fluctuations in the pitch of someone's voice, rapid changes in conversation topics, changes in mood, underlying humor, and sarcasm. This makes your ability to orally communicate with another person extremely valuable. It cannot be outsourced or automated. Yet most people completely ignore this critical skill—especially in today's world. Understand that the best oral communicators always rise to the top. If you improve your speaking skills, you will generate more influence. You can then use this influence to help you fulfill your purpose in life.

Take physical action

Without action, ideas rot. Great ideas are a dime a dozen—here today, gone today. Everyone has a great idea, but the only way to bring that idea to life is through physical action. There are trillions of ideas floating around but less than 0.001% of those ideas will be made into a service or product. It can take an entire lifetime to turn even one simple idea into a physical reality. In fact, it can take several people, several lifetimes. And there are only seven billion people on the planet. This is why taking massive action towards your goals, or towards bringing your ideas to life, is so important.

Our bodies and brains are built for action. If you want your body to continue to work properly, you have to stay active. The same holds true for your brain. In *Brain Rules*, Dr John Medina tells how our brains developed to work optimally alongside physical activity, citing how our ancestors walked an average of 12 miles a day.[40] The human brain loves oxygen and works best when the body is taking physical action. Physical action helps pump oxygen into the lungs, through the bloodstream, and into the brain. This is why large estates used to have pacing rooms, where the lord of the manor would walk in circles while thinking and dictating his ideas. Physical action will always be required for turning an abstract thought into a physical reality.

Choose the right idea

Mental choice is your most valuable skill. Your decisions will determine what you experience and accomplish in life. Most importantly, your choices will determine how you experience life. When I travel to give seminars and speeches, I dictate and send my emails with Siri,[41] I have all of my Facebook[42] messages, tweets,[43] emails, texts, and phone calls forwarded to Talkatone,[44] I have my voice mails automatically transcribed and emailed to me with Google Voice,[45] I automatically upload business cards to my phone contacts with WorldCard,[46] I automatically download my receipts and generate expense reports with Expensify,[47] I keep a daily journal

The only human skill that will never be automatic is mental choice.

with Evernote,[48] and I save all my songs, videos, and pictures on iCloud.[49] Thanks to all of the different apps and software programs that allow you to store, organize, and transfer information in cyberspace, everything is becoming automatic.

The only human skill that will never be automatic is mental choice. Human beings will always have to program, or tell, computers what choices to make. Mental choice is a uniquely human skill. Your mental choices direct your focus and determine your attitude. Everything else in life is secondary. This is why philosophers have debated the question of whether free will exists for centuries. Free will is defined as the ability to make choices without the constraint of necessity or fate. In other words, it's the ability to act at one's own discretion. You can think of free will as the influence you have over your own future. Yet most people allow external circumstances to determine their attitude and focus, which causes them to enter a state of mental disorder.

Your mental choices direct your focus and determine your attitude. Everything else in life is secondary.

In the book *Flow*, Dr Mihaly Csikszentmihalyi writes about how your emotions are actually internal states of consciousness.[50] Negative emotions such as fear, anxiety, or boredom produce "psychic entropy," a state in which you cannot use your attention effectively to deal with external tasks. Conversely, positive emotions such as enjoyment and alertness produce "psychic negentropy," a state where psychic energy can flow freely into whatever task or thought you choose to invest in. Maintaining a state of psychic negentropy is critical to making good decisions throughout your life. If you start sinking into a state of psychic entropy, simply remember that you are in control of your focus. Remember to think inside the box and move laterally. Remember that you can manipulate reality for the better at will.

Conclusion

The most empowering moment of your life will occur when you realize you are completely in control of your attention, attitude, and, ultimately, decisions. Anything that happens to you in life is up for interpretation. And it's your perspective that will determine how you interpret what happens.

Here's the key: you get to *choose* your perspective. You also get to choose your actions. This means that it's your choices, above all else, that will determine what happens to you in life. It's your choices that will determine your purpose and whether or not you fulfill it. The person you are today is a direct result of your choices. The future belongs to those who can make the best choices. The future belongs to those who choose to break free, think strategically, and create a more powerful purpose for their life.

Create a powerful purpose

Finding your purpose is a matter of life and death; it is also your escape plan. Purpose prevents mediocrity and meaninglessness. The only way to fulfill a worthwhile purpose for your life is to focus on what is causing you pain, and then make a decision to never experience that pain again. Energize your purpose by ruthlessly evaluating your current position and creating a detailed vision of the future position that you want to achieve. Then, work backwards to connect the two.

The end point of your purpose in life is not a job title or an annual salary. Your end point is the wish list of actions that you want to wake up and do on a daily basis. The only way to achieve a lifestyle that will allow these actions is actively define your core priorities. Combined with a strong purpose, your core priorities have an irresistible force over your life. Add to this force by using short-term benchmarks and positive storytelling. Realize that you will never fulfill a good purpose by living out a bad story. Take time to deconstruct your old life story and to write a new life story that matches your new purpose.

Next, create a personal slogan, a meme, and a list of empowering questions. Remember, you can change your focus and perspective at any time, simply by changing the questions you're asking yourself. The final step of finding your purpose is to create and display a vision board that exposes your very deepest desires. You will know that you've found your purpose when you have a concrete vision of it in front of you. Once you have your vision, turn it into a decision and back it with conviction.

Fulfill your new purpose

Achieving a worthy purpose will require a lot of effort: 10,000 hours, to be exact. There's no way to eliminate this time count, but you can reduce it by practicing the arts of association, convergence, metamorphosis, automation, ritualization, and adjustment. Be careful to avoid the effects of willpower depletion and to avoid believing in the life hack lie. How-to lists and get-rich-quick schemes will not fulfill you.

Fulfillment is simply a matter of making the right investments. Make sure you invest the majority of your time, energy, and money in yourself and in other people. Build strong relationships, but also build a strong identity. Connect massively but don't get lost in the crowd.

As you begin to fulfill your purpose, make sure that you attack any limiting beliefs that crop up right away. Limiting beliefs are the only things that will stop you from achieving your biggest goals in life. Remember, you don't have to give up anything in order to get everything you've ever wanted. Your new purpose can be your new reality. All you have to do is stay strategic, stay flexible, and keep taking action in the right direction.

Special Bonus

If you would like raw materials for the case studies and exercises in this book, along with the research articles I gathered, I'd like to send them to you.

All you need to do is email me here:

isaiahhankel@gmail.com

I will also send you the first step of my program, *The Escape Plan*^{TM}, which shows you how to escape from mediocrity by building a successful business around your purpose. As a bonus, I'll give you a redemption code to receive a chapter from *GO NAKED: Revealing the Secrets of Successful Selling*, a book written by Michael Smith (see Michael's case study on page 194).

Notes

Preface

1 For more information on PhD tenure rates, see http://www. nature.com/naturejobs/science/articles/10.1038/nj7320-123a

2 For more information on grant funding rates in the US, see http://report.nih.gov/success_rates/

Part One

1 Buettner, D. (2008) *The Blue Zones: Lessons for Living Longer from the People Who've Lived the Longest,* National Geographic Society, Washington, DC.

2 Tsai, S., Wendt, J., Donnelly, R., de Jong, G. & Ahmed, F. (2005) "Age at Retirement and Long Term Survival of an Industrial Population: Prospective Cohort Study," *BMJ* 331. http://www.bmj.com/content/331/7523/995

3 Rush University Medical Center (2012) "Greater Purpose in Life May Protect against Harmful Changes in the Brain Associated with Alzheimer's Disease," *Science Daily,* http://www.sciencedaily.com/releases/2012/05/120507164326.htm

4 O'Callaghan, T. (2010) "Sense of Fulfillment Linked to Lower Alzheimer's Risk," *Time Health & Family,* http://healthland.time.com/2010/03/01/ sense-of-fulfillment-linked-to-lower-alzheimers-risk/

5   Doheny, K. (2009) "Have a Purpose in Life? You Might Live Longer," *Health*, http://news.health.com/2009/06/16/have-purpose-life-you-might-live-longer/

6   Robbins, A. (1992) *Awaken the Giant Within: How to Take Immediate Control of Your Mental, Emotional, Physical and Financial Destiny!* Simon & Schuster Free Press, New York, NY.

7   Hemingway, E. (1952) *The Old Man and the Sea*, http://www.goodreads.com/quotes/304776-a-man-can-be-destroyed-but-not-defeated

8   Hanson, R. (2013) *Hardwiring Happiness: The New Brain Science of Contentment, Calm, and Confidence*, Random House, New York, NY.

9   Kelley, K. (2010) *Oprah: A Biography*, Random House New York, NY.

10 For more information on Leonardo Del Vecchio and Luxottica, see http://www.businessinsider.com/rags-to-riches-stories-2011-11?op=1

11 Walton, S. & Huey, J. (1992) *Sam Walton: Made in America*, Doubleday, New York, NY.

12 For more information on J.K. Rowling and the Harry Potter series of books, see http://www.biography.com/people/jk-rowling-40998?page=1

13 http://www.psychosomaticmedicine.org/content/19/3/191.full.pdf

14 Walton, N. (2009) *Ultra-Fat to Ultra-Fit: A Scientist's Rational Approach to Extreme Weight Loss and Optimal Fitness*, Sentient, Boulder, CO.

15 Farmer, E. (2012) *Breaking In: The Formula for Success in Entertainment*, ISB Publishing, Dallas, TX.

16 Kitchen, J. (2006) *Writing a Great Movie: Key Tools for Successful Screenwriting*, Lone Eagle Publishing Company, New York, NY.

17 For more information on *The Secret*, see http://thesecret.tv/

18 For more information on the Dominican University goal study, see http://www.dominican.edu/dominicannews/ study-backs-up-strategies-for-achieving-goals

19 For more information on the Virginia Tech goal study, see http://www.goalsgonesocial.com/ggs2/blogs/write_down_goals

Part Two

1 Greene, R. & 50 Cent (2009) *The 50th Law*, HarperCollins, New York, NY.

2 US News & World Report (2013) *Best Law Schools, US News*, http://grad-schools.usnews.rankingsandreviews.com/ best-graduate-schools/top-law-schools/law-rankings

3 Mailer, N. & McCann, C. (2010) *MoonFire: The Epic Journey of Apollo 11*, Taschen America, LLC, Los Angeles, CA.

4 Hensley, D. (2012) *From the Edge of Space*, Kindle edition. For more information on Baumgartner, see http://www. dailymail.co.uk/news/article-2218268/Felix-Baumgartner-Thought-plummeting-24-miles-834mph-crazy-Just-read-hes-to. html

5 Hawking, S. (2011) *A Brief History of Time: From Big Bang to Black Hole*, Bantam, New York, NY.

6 Nourse, J. (1981) *The Simple Solution to Rubik's Cube*, Bantam, New York, NY.

7 For more information on what Crossfit is, see http://www. crossfit.com/

8 US News & World Report (2014) "Best Business Schools," *US News*, http://grad-schools.usnews.rankingsandreviews. com/best-graduate-schools/top-business-schools/ mba-rankings?int=acf0d6

9 For more information on Amgen and the Fortune 500 list, see http://money.cnn.com/magazines/fortune/fortune500/2013/ full_list/index.html?iid=F500_sp_full

10 Haven, K. (2007) *Story Proof: The Science behind the Startling Power of Story*, Libraries Unlimited, Westport, CT.

11 Fields, R.D. (2010) "Of Two Minds: Listener Brain Patterns Mirror Those of the Speaker," *Scientific American*, http://blogs.scientificamerican.com/guest-blog/2010/07/27/of-two-minds-listener-brain-patterns-mirror-those-of-the-speaker/

12 McIntyre, K. (2011) "Storytelling Program Improves Lives of People with ALZHEIMER'S: Creative Intervention Bolsters Well-Being, MU Researchers Find," University of Missouri News Bureau, http://munews.missouri.edu/news-releases/2011/0223-storytelling-program-improves-lives-of-people-with-alzheimer%E2%80%99s/

13 White, M. & Epston, D. (1990) *Narrative Means to Therapeutic Ends*, W.W. Norton, New York, NY.

14 Vromans, L. & Schweitzer, R. (2010) "Narrative Therapy for Adults with a Major Depressive Disorder: Improved Symptom and Interpersonal Outcomes," *Psychotherapy Research*, http://www.dulwichcentre.com.au/narrative-therapy-research.html

15 Weber, M., Davis, K. & McPhie, L. (2006) "Narrative Therapy, Eating Disorders and Groups: Enhancing Outcomes in Rural NSW," *Australian Social Work* 59(4):391–405, http://www.ingentaconnect.com/content/routledg/asw/2006/00000059/00000004/art00004

16 For more information on *Rocky*, see http://www.imdb.com/title/tt0075148/

17 For more information about the J. Robinson Intensive Wrestling Camp, see http://jrobinsoncamps.com/

18 For more information on the movies referenced in this paragraph, see http://www.imdb.com/

19 For more information about the Uganda Village Project, see http://www.ugandavillageproject.org/

20 For more information about Chester Santos, see http://www.internationalmanofmemory.com/

21 For more information on the USA Memory Championship, see http://www.usamemorychampionship.com/

22 Covey, S. (2004) *The 7 Habits of Highly Effective People: Powerful Lessons in Personal Change*, Free Press, New York, NY.

23 Bell, J. (2011) "Why Mission Statements Suck," *CEO Afterlife*, http://www.ceoafterlife.com/leadership/why-mission-statements-suck-2/

24 Harvard University, "What is Harvard's Mission Statement?" http://www.harvard.edu/faqs/mission-statement

25 Wikipedia. "Meme." http://en.wikipedia.org/wiki/Meme.

26 Duhigg, C. (2012) *The Power of Habit: Why We Do What We Do in Life and Business*, Random House, New York, NY.

27 Osteen, J. (2004) *Your Best Life Now: 7 Steps for Living at Your Full Potential*, FaithWords, New York, NY.

28 Wasmund, S. (2011) *Stop Talking, Start Doing: A Kick in the Pants in Six Parts*, Capstone Publishing, Chichester, UK.

29 Bradford Cannon, W. (2002) "'Voodoo' Death," *American Journal of Public Health*, 92(10):1593–6, http://www.ncbi.nlm.nih.gov/pmc/articles/PMC1447285/

30 For more information on "voodoo" deaths, see http://en.wikipedia.org/wiki/Voodoo_death

31 Moseley, J., O'Malley, K., et al. (2002) "A Controlled Trial of Arthroscopic Surgery for Osteoarthritis of the Knee," *The New England Journal of Medicine*, 347:81–8 http://www.nejm.org/doi/full/10.1056/NEJMoa013259#t=article

32 Willis, M. (2002) "Knee Surgery No Better Than Placebo," ABC News, http://abcnews.go.com/Health/story?id=116879&page=1

33 Tauber, R. (1997) *Self-Fulfilling Prophecy: A Practical Guide to its Use in Education*, Praeger Publishers, Westport, CT.

34 Rosenthal, R. & Jacobson, L. (1968) *Pygmalion in the Classroom: Teacher Expectation and Pupils' Intellectual Development*, Holt, Rinehart & Winston New York, NY.

35 For more information on *Rudy*, see http://www.imdb.com/title/tt0108002/

36 For more information on *The Pursuit of Happyness*, see http://www.imdb.com/title/tt0454921/

37 Ferriss, T. (2007) *The 4-Hour Workweek: Escape 9–5, Live Anywhere, and Join the New Rich*, Crown Publishers, New York, NY.

Part Three

1 For more information on Kaplan Test Prep courses, see http://www.kaptest.com/MCAT/Home/index.html

2 Gladwell, M. (2008) *Outliers: The Story of Success*, Little, Brown and Company, Boston, MA.

3 Colvin, G. (2008) *Talent Is Overrated: What Really Separates World-Class Performers from Everybody Else*, Portfolio, New York, NY.

4 Sullivan, B. (2013) *The Plateau Effect: Getting from Stuck to Success*, Dutton Adult, New York, NY.

5 Godin, S. (2008) *Tribes: We Need You to Lead Us*, Portfolio, New York, NY.

6 Greene, R. (2012) *Mastery*, Viking, New York, NY.

7 Duhigg, op. cit.

8 Gailliot, M., Baumeister, R., et al. (2007) "Self-Control Relies on Glucose as a Limited Energy Source: Willpower is More Than a Metaphor," *Journal of Personality and Social Psychology* 92(2):325–36, http://www.fed.cuhk.edu.hk/~lchang/material/Evolutionary/Brain/Self-control%20relies%20on%20glucose%20as%20a%20limited%20

energy%20source%20willpower%20Is%20more%20
than%20a%20metaphor.pdf

9 For more information on Burning Man, see
http://www.burningman.com/

10 For more information on the sermon on Mount Sinai, see:
http://www.biblegateway.com/passage/?search=Exodus+19&ve
rsion=NIV.

11 Check out my blog at http://www.isaiahhankel.com/.

12 Godin, S. 2007. *The Dip: A Little Book that Teaches You
When to Quit*. New York, NY: Portfolio.

13 Lehrer, J. 2010. *How We Decide*. New York, NY: Houghton
Mifflin.

14 For more information on the Academy of General Dentistry,
see http://www.agd.org/publications-media/publications/
general-dentistry.aspx.

15 For more information on the Marshmallow Challenge, see
http://marshmallowchallenge.com/Welcome.html.

16 Wasmund, op. cit.

17 Heath, D. and Heath, C. 2008. *Made to Stick: Why Some
Ideas Take Hold and Others Come Unstuck*. London, UK:
Random House.

18 Robbins, op. cit.

19 Wikipedia. "HTTP cookie." http://en.wikipedia.org/wiki/
HTTP_cookie.

20 Kaufman, J. 2012. *The Personal MBA: Master the Art of
Business*. New York, NY: Portfolio.

21 Pink, D. 2009. *Drive: The Surprising Truth about What
Motivates Us*. New York, NY: Riverhead Books.

22 For more information on Vygon, see https://www.vygon.com/
en/.

23 For more information on Johnson & Johnson, see http://www. jnj.com/.

24 For more information on the Warwick Business School's MBA program, see http://www.wbs.ac.uk/.

25 For more information on the Henley Business School's Executive Coaching program, see http://www.henley.ac.uk/.

26 For more information on "Go Naked: Revealing the Secrets of Powerful Relationships", see http://www.gonakedselling.com/.

27 For more information on Silverwood theme park, see: http:// www.silverwoodthemepark.com/.

28 Kaufman, op. cit.

29 For more information on Elance, see https://www.elance.com/.

30 For more information on the Academy of Management, see http://aom.org/amj/.

31 Wolff, H. and Moser, M. 2009. "Effects of Networking on Career Success: A Longitudinal Study." *Journal of Applied Psychology* 94(1), 196–206. http://www.ncbi.nlm.nih.gov/ pubmed/19186904.

32 For more information on current referral and hiring statistics, see http://www.ere.net/2012/05/07/10-compelling-numbers-that-reveal-the-power-of-employee-referrals/.

33 For more information on Angie's List, see http://www. angieslist.com/.

34 For more information on escalator pitches, see http:// www.businessweek.com/stories/2008-05-16/the-escalator-pitchbusinessweek-business-news-stock-market-and-financial-advice.

35 For more information on my company, Cheeky Scientist: Personal Development for Intelligent People, see http:// cheekyscientist.com/.

36 Christopher, J. 2011. *Microstyle: The Art of Writing Little.* New York, NY: Norton & Company.

37 For more information on the movies referenced in this paragraph, see http://www.imdb.com/.

38 For more information on Ideafarms, see http://ideafarms.com/.

39 For more information on IdeaConnection, see http://www. ideaconnection.com/.

40 Medina, J. 2009. *Brain Rules: 12 Principles for Surviving and Thriving at Work, Home, and School.* Seattle, WA: Pear Press.

41 For more information on Siri, see http://www.apple.com/ios/siri/.

42 See my Facebook page at https://www.facebook.com/isaiahhankelphd.

43 See my Twitter page at https://twitter.com/isaiahhankel.

44 For more information about Talkatone, see http://www.talkatone.com/.

45 For more information about Google Voice, see http://www.google.com/googlevoice/about.html.

46 For more information about WorldCard, see http://worldcard.penpowerinc.com/product.asp?sn=158.

47 For more information about Expensify, see https://www.expensify.com/.

48 For more information about Evernote, see http://evernote.com/.

49 For more information about iCloud, see http://www.apple.com/icloud/.

50 Csikszentmihalyi, M. 2009. *Flow: The Psychology of Optimal Experience.* New York, NY: HarperCollins.

About the Author

Doctor and Fortune 500 consultant Isaiah Hankel is an internationally recognized expert in the biotechnology industry who specializes in helping businesses transition into cutting-edge, entrepreneurship-driven markets.

Isaiah has worked with some of the world's leading corporations, including Amgen, Celgene, Baxter Bioscience, Pfizer, Roche, and Genentech. He has also presented at many of the world's premier academic institutions, including Harvard University, Stanford University, Oxford University, Cambridge University, and the Pasteur and Curie Institutes in Paris.

Long before getting his PhD in Anatomy and Cell Biology, Isaiah worked as a sheep farmer and lived in rural Idaho where he struggled in school and was repeatedly diagnosed with ADD and ADHD. He survived college and barely made it into graduate school where he was quickly put on academic probation and forced to work as a janitor and sleep in a friend's basement to get by. Less than three years later, Isaiah formed three successful, multinational businesses and started managing a multimillion dollar product line. He also became a prolific public speaker, giving more than 250 seminars in 22 different countries.

The system Isaiah used to go from being an ADD-diagnosed sheep farmer to a being a successful entrepreneur, author, and business coach is carefully laid out in this book and in his live presentations. Isaiah mixes science, strategy, and entertaining personal stories to empower people while providing them with actionable takeaways that they can immediately use to improve their focus and performance.

Index

Index